Grammar Links 2

A Theme-Based Course for Reference and Practice

Volume A

SECOND EDITION

M. Kathleen Mahnke
Saint Michael's College

Elizabeth O'Dowd
Saint Michael's College

M. Kathleen Mahnke
Series Editor

Houghton Mifflin Company   Boston   New York

Publisher: Patricia A. Coryell
Director of ESL: Susan Maguire
Senior Development Editor: Kathleen Sands Boehmer
Editorial Assistant: Evangeline Bermas
Senior Project Editor: Margaret Park Bridges
Senior Manufacturing Coordinator: Marie Barnes
Marketing Manager: Annamarie Rice
Marketing Associate: Laura Hemrika

Printed in the U.S.A.

Library of Congress Control Number: 2003115072

ISBN: 0-618-27417-0

23456789-HES-08 07 06

Contents

Introduction   v

UNIT ONE   **Present Time**   1
Topic Focus: People and Personalities

Chapter 1:   **Simple Present Tense; Adverbs of Frequency**   4
Grammar Briefing 1: Simple Present Tense I   5
Grammar Briefing 2: Simple Present Tense II   9
Grammar Briefing 3: Adverbs of Frequency with the   13
    Simple Present Tense

Chapter 2:   **Present Progressive Tense**   18
Grammar Briefing 1: Present Progressive Tense I   20
Grammar Briefing 2: Present Progressive Tense II   22
Grammar Briefing 3: Present Progressive Tense III   25

Chapter 3:   **Simple Present and Present Progressive**   30
Grammar Briefing 1: Simple Present Versus   31
    Present Progressive
Grammar Briefing 2: Verbs with Stative Meaning   34

UNIT TWO   **Past Time**   45
Topic Focus: Unsolved Mysteries

Chapter 4:   **Simple Past Tense; *Used To***   48
Grammar Briefing 1: Simple Past Tense I   49
Grammar Briefing 2: Simple Past Tense II   54
Grammar Briefing 3: *Used To*   57

Chapter 5:   **Past Progressive Tense; Simple Past and   62
Past Progressive; Past Time Clauses**
Grammar Briefing 1: Past Progressive Tense I   63
Grammar Briefing 2: Past Progressive Tense II   65
Grammar Briefing 3: Simple Past Tense Versus   68
    Past Progressive Tense
Grammar Briefing 4: Past Time Clauses with   73
    When and *While*

| UNIT THREE | **Future Time** | **85** |
| | Topic Focus: Living with Technology | |

Chapter 6:	**Expressing Future Time**	**88**
	Grammar Briefing 1: Future Time with *Be Going To* I	89
	Grammar Briefing 2: Future Time with *Be Going To* II	94
	Grammar Briefing 3: Future Time with *Will* I	97
	Grammar Briefing 4: Future Time with *Will* II	99
	Grammar Briefing 5: *Be Going To* Versus *Will*	105
	Grammar Briefing 6: Present Progressive and Simple Present for Future Time	107

Chapter 7:	**Future Time Clauses; Conditionals**	**114**
	Grammar Briefing 1: Future Time Clauses	115
	Grammar Briefing 2: Factual and Future Conditionals	122

| UNIT FOUR | **Nouns, Articles, Quantifiers, and Pronouns** | **133** |
| | Topic Focus: Travel and Transportation | |

Chapter 8:	**Nouns and Articles**	**136**
	Grammar Briefing 1: Proper Nouns and Common Nouns	138
	Grammar Briefing 2: Count and Noncount Nouns	141
	Grammar Briefing 3: The Indefinite Article *A/An*	148
	Grammar Briefing 4: The Definite Article *The*	151

Chapter 9:	**General Quantifiers; Numbers; Measure Words**	**156**
	Grammar Briefing 1: General Quantifiers I	158
	Grammar Briefing 2: General Quantifiers II	160
	Grammar Briefing 3: Numbers and Measure Words	167

Chapter 10:	**Pronouns and Possessives**	**171**
	Grammar Briefing 1: Pronouns and Possessive Adjectives I	172
	Grammar Briefing 2: Pronouns and Possessive Adjectives II	173
	Grammar Briefing 3: Indefinite Pronouns	182

	Appendixes	**A-1**
	Grammar Glossary	**A-14**
	Index	**A-18**

Introduction

WELCOME TO *GRAMMAR LINKS*!

Grammar Links is a comprehensive five-level grammar reference and practice series for students of English as a second or foreign language. The series meets the needs of students from the beginning through advanced levels:

- *Grammar Links Basic*: beginning
- *Grammar Links, Book 1*: high beginning
- *Grammar Links, Book 2*: intermediate
- *Grammar Links, Book 3*: high intermediate
- *Grammar Links, Book 4*: advanced

Available with each *Grammar Links* student text are an audio program and printable Web-based teacher's notes; the teacher's notes are accompanied by the answer key and tapescripts for each book. Tests and other materials are also available on the Houghton Mifflin Website and are described below. In addition, *Grammar Links 1–4* feature workbooks for further practice of all grammar points introduced in the student books.

NEW IN THIS EDITION

- A fresh, new design with eye-catching art, realia, and a focus on ease of use
- Streamlined, easy-to-read grammar charts showing structures at a glance
- Succinct explanations of grammar points for easy understanding
- Simplified content coverage accompanied by vocabulary glosses to let students focus on grammar while learning about topics of interest
- An even greater number and variety of activities than before, now signaled with icons for easy reference:

    Listening activities for receptive practice of grammar structures in oral English

    Communicative activities that lead to fluent use of grammar in everyday speaking

    Writing activities for productive practice of targeted structures in extended written discourse

    Links to the World Wide Web for:
    - Model paragraphs for writing assignments
    - Practice tests, both self-check tests for student use and achievement tests for teacher use
    - Links to interesting sites related to unit themes for further reading and discussion
    - Vocabulary flashcards for review of the content-related vocabulary that is used in text readings and exercises
    - Much more! See for yourself at www.hmco.com/college/esl.

Series Approach

Recent research in applied linguistics tells us that when a well-designed communicative approach is coupled with a systematic treatment of grammatical form, the combination is a powerful pedagogical tool.

Grammar Links is such a tool. The grammar explanations in *Grammar Links* are clear, accurate, and carefully sequenced. All points that are introduced are practiced in exercises, and coverage is comprehensive and systematic. In addition, each grammar point is carefully recycled in a variety of contexts.

The communicative framework of *Grammar Links* is that of the theme-based approach to language learning. Unlike other approaches, theme-based models promote the development of both communicative and linguistic abilities through in-depth contextualization of language in extended discourse. The importance of this type of contextualization to grammar acquisition is now well documented. In *Grammar Links*, content serves as a backdrop for communication; high-interest topics are presented and developed along with the grammar of each chapter. As a result, *Grammar Links* exercises and activities are content-driven as well as grammar-driven. While learning about adjective clauses in Book 3, for example, students explore various aspects of the discipline of psychology. While they are practicing gerunds and infinitives in Book 2, they read about successful American entrepreneurs. And while practicing the simple present tense in Book 1, students learn about and discuss North American festivals and other celebrations. Throughout the series, students communicate about meaningful content, transferring their grammatical training to the English they need in their daily lives.

Complementing the communicative theme-based approach of the *Grammar Links* series is the inclusion of a range of successful methodological options for exercises and activities. In addition to more traditional, explicit rule presentation and practice, we have incorporated a number of less explicit, more inductive techniques. Foremost among these are our discovery exercises and activities, in which students are asked to notice general and specific grammatical features and think about them on their own, sometimes formulating their own hypotheses about how these features work and why they work the way they do. Discovery exercises are included in each unit opener. They are frequently used in chapter openers as well and are interspersed throughout the *Grammar Practice* sections, particularly at the higher levels.

In short, the *Grammar Links* approach provides students with the best of all possible language learning environments—a comprehensive, systematic treatment of grammar that employs a variety of methods for grammar learning within a communicative theme-based framework.

About the Books

Each book in the *Grammar Links* series is divided into approximately 10 units. Each unit looks at a well-defined area of grammar, and each unit has an overall theme. The chapters within a unit each focus on some part of the targeted unit grammar, and each chapter develops some specific aspect of the unit theme. In this way, chapters in a unit are linked in terms of both grammar coverage and theme, providing a highly contextualized base on which students can build and refine their grammatical skills.

Grammar coverage has been carefully designed to spiral across levels. Structures that are introduced in one book are recycled and built upon in the next. Students not only learn increasingly sophisticated information about the structures but also practice these structures in increasingly challenging contexts. Themes show a similar progression across levels, from less academic in Books 1 and 2 to more academic in Books 3 and 4.

Grammar Links is flexible in many ways and can be easily adapted to the particular needs of users. Although its careful spiraling makes it ideal as a series, the comprehensive grammar coverage at each level means that the individual books can also stand alone. The comprehensiveness and careful organization also make it possible for students to use their text as a reference after they have completed a course. The units in a book can be used in the order given or can be rearranged to fit the teacher's curriculum. Books can be used in their entirety or in part. In addition, the inclusion of ample practice allows teachers to be selective when choosing exercises and activities. All exercises are labeled for grammatical content, so structures can be practiced more or less extensively, depending on class and individual needs.

Unit and Chapter Components

■ **Unit Objectives.** Each unit begins with a list of unit objectives so that teachers and students can preview the major grammar points covered in the unit. Objectives are accompanied by example sentences, which highlight the relevant structures.

■ **Unit Introduction.** To illustrate grammar use in extended discourse, a reading and listening selection introduces both the unit grammar and the unit theme in a unit opener section entitled *Grammar in Action.* This material is followed by a grammar consciousness-raising or "noticing" task, *Think About Grammar.* In *Think About Grammar* tasks, students figure out some aspect of grammar by looking at words and sentences from the *Grammar in Action* selection, often working together to answer questions about them. Students induce grammatical rules themselves before having those rules given to them. *Think About Grammar* thus helps students to become independent grammar learners by promoting critical thinking and discussion about grammar.

■ **Chapter Introduction.** Each chapter opens with a task. This task involves students in working receptively with the structures that are treated in the chapter and gives them the opportunity to begin thinking about the chapter theme.

■ *Grammar Briefings.* The grammar is presented in *Grammar Briefings.* Chapters generally have three or four *Grammar Briefings* so that information is given in manageable chunks. The core of each *Grammar Briefing* is its **form** and **function** charts. In these charts, the form (the *what* of grammar) and the function (the *how, when,* and *why*) are presented in logical segments. These segments are manageable but large enough that students can see connections between related grammar points. Form and function are presented in separate charts when appropriate but together when the two are essentially inseparable. All grammatical descriptions in the form and function charts are comprehensive, concise, and clear. Sample sentences illustrate each point.

■ *Grammar Hotspots.* *Grammar Hotspots* are a special feature of *Grammar Links.* They occur at one or more strategic points in each chapter. *Grammar Hotspots* focus on aspects of grammar that students are likely to find particularly troublesome. Some hotspots contain reminders about material that has already been presented in the form and function charts; others go beyond the charts.

■ *Talking the Talk.* *Talking the Talk* is another special feature of the *Grammar Links* series. Our choice of grammar is often determined by our audience, whether we are writing or speaking, the situations in which we find ourselves, and other sociocultural factors. *Talking the Talk* treats these factors. Students become aware of differences between formal and informal English, between written and spoken English.

■ *Grammar Practice.* Each *Grammar Briefing* is followed by comprehensive and systematic practice of all grammar points introduced. The general progression within each *Grammar Practice* is from more controlled to less controlled, from easier to more difficult, and often from more receptive to more productive and/or more structured to more communicative. A wide variety of innovative exercise types is included in each of the four skill areas: listening, speaking, reading, and writing. The exercise types that are used are appropriate to the particular grammar points being practiced. For example, more drill-like exercises are often used for practice with form. More open-ended exercises often focus on function.

In many cases, drill-like practice of a particular grammar point is followed by open-ended communicative practice of the same point, often as pair or group work. Thus, a number of exercises have two parts.

The majority of exercises within each *Grammar Practice* section are related to the theme of the unit. However, some exercises depart from the theme to ensure that each grammar point is practiced in the most effective way.

■ **Unit Wrap-Ups.** Each unit ends with a series of activities that pull the unit grammar together and enable students to test, further practice, and apply what they have learned. These activities include an error correction task, which covers the errors students most commonly make in using the structures presented in the unit, as well as a series of innovative open-ended communicative tasks, which build on and go beyond the individual chapters.

■ **Appendixes.** Extensive appendixes supplement the grammar presented in the *Grammar Briefings.* They provide students with word lists, spelling and pronunciation rules, and other supplemental rules related to the structures that have been taught. The appendixes are a rich resource for students as they work through exercises and activities.

■ **Grammar Glossary.** A grammar glossary provides students and teachers with definitions of the grammar terms used in *Grammar Links* as well as example sentences to aid in understanding the meaning of each term.

Other Components

■ **Audio Program.** All *Grammar Links* listening exercises and all unit introductions are recorded on audio CDs and cassettes. The symbol 🎧 appears next to the title of each recorded segment.

■ **Workbook.** *Grammar Links 1–4* student texts are each accompanied by a workbook. The four workbooks contain a wide variety of exercise types, including paragraph and essay writing, and they provide extensive supplemental self-study practice of each grammar point presented in the student texts. Student self-tests with TOEFL® practice questions are also included in the workbooks.

■ **Teacher's Notes.** The *Grammar Links* teacher's notes for each student text can be downloaded from <http://www.hmco.com/college/esl/>. Each contains an introduction to the series and some general and specific teaching guidelines.

■ **Tapescript and Answer Keys.** The tapescript and the answer key for the student text and the answer key for the workbook are also available at the *Grammar Links* Website.

■ **Links to the World Wide Web.** As was discussed above, the *Grammar Links* Website www.hmco.com/college/esl/ has been expanded for the second edition to include student and teacher tests, teacher notes, model writing assignments, content Web links and activities, and other material. Links are updated frequently to ensure that students and teachers can access the best information available on the Web.

TO THE STUDENT

Grammar Links is a five-level series that gives you all the rules and practice you need to learn and use English grammar. Each unit in this book focuses on an area of grammar. Each unit also develops a theme—for example, business or travel. Units are divided into two or three chapters.

Grammar Links has many special features that will help you to learn the grammar and to use it in speaking, listening, reading, and writing.

FEATURE	BENEFIT
Interesting Themes	Help you link grammar to the real world—the world of everyday English
Introductory Reading and Listening Selections	Introduce you to the theme and the grammar of the unit
Think About Grammar Activities	Help you to become an independent grammar learner
Chapter Opener Tasks	Get you started using the grammar
Grammar Briefings	Give you clear grammar rules in easy-to-read charts, with helpful example sentences
Grammar Hotspots	Focus on especially difficult grammar points for learners of English—points on which you might want to spend extra time
Talking the Talk	Helps you to understand the differences between formal and informal English and between written and spoken English
Grammar Practice	Gives you lots of practice, through listening, speaking, reading, and writing exercises and activities
Unit Wrap-Up Tasks	Provide you with interesting communicative activities that cover everything you have learned in the unit
Vocabulary Glosses	Define key words in readings and exercises so that you can concentrate on your grammar practice while still learning about interesting content
Grammar Glossary	Gives you definitions and example sentences for the most common words used to talk about English grammar—a handy reference for now and for later
Websites	Guide you to more information about topics of interest
	Provide you with self-tests with immediate correction and feedback, vocabulary flashcards for extra practice with words that might be new to you, models for writing assignments, and extra practice exercises

All of these features combine to make *Grammar Links* interesting and rewarding—and, I hope, FUN!

M. Kathleen Mahnke, Series Editor
Saint Michael's College
Colchester, VT USA

ACKNOWLEDGMENTS

Series Editor Acknowledgments

This edition of *Grammar Links* would not have been possible without the thoughtful and enthusiastic feedback of teachers and students. Many thanks to you all!

I would also like to thank all of the *Grammar Links* authors, from whom I continue to learn so much every day. Many thanks as well to the dedicated staff at Houghton Mifflin: Joann Kozyrev, Evangeline Bermas, and Annamarie Rice.

A very special thanks to Kathy Sands Boehmer and to Susan Maguire for their vision, their sense of humor, their faith in all of us, their flexibility, their undying tenacity, and their willingness to take risks in order to move from the mundane to the truly inspirational.

Author Acknowledgments

We would like to express our appreciation to the following individuals who helped to make this book possible:

Our valiant editor, Karen Davy, who worried, teased, and stretched our efforts toward a product we could be proud of.

The staff at Houghton Mifflin for their constant patience and encouragement.

The other *Grammar Links* series authors for their commitment and their camaraderie.

Our friends and colleagues at Saint Michael's College, who provided support in their invaluable ways.

In addition, we are grateful to the following members of the revision advisory board:

Marianne Grayston, Prince George's Community College
Cristi Mitchell, Miami-Dade Community College
Terry Robinson, University of Texas, Brownsville
Oscar Vera, University of Texas, Brownsville

Finally, our warmest gratitude goes to our close families and friends for feeding, sustaining, and worrying about us through the writing and production process: Wayne Parker, Greg Mahnke, Paddy and Mary O'Dowd, the Olivers of La Luz, New Mexico, and, last but not least, Tina, Amelia, and Cosmo.

Thanks, one and all!
M. Kathleen Mahnke and Elizabeth O'Dowd

Present Time

TOPIC FOCUS
People and Personalities

UNIT OBJECTIVES

■ **the simple present tense**
(George *lives* alone. He *doesn't make* friends easily.)

■ **adverbs of frequency with the simple present tense**
(You *often* talk about your personality. You're *always* happy.)

■ **the present progressive tense**
(I *am* not *enjoying* my job. I*'m looking for* a new job.)

■ **choosing between the simple present and the present progressive**
(They usually *worry* a lot. They *aren't worrying* today.)

■ **verbs with stative meaning**
(Kim *likes* parties. She *has* an outgoing personality.)

Grammar in Action

🎧 Reading and Listening: Good Stress, Bad Stress

Professor Larson is giving a class lecture about people and personalities.
Read and listen.

Good morning, class. Today we are starting a new topic. The topic is stress. Stress is our response to a threat or a new situation. The world is changing very fast, and there are always new threats and new situations. So stress is becoming a problem for all of us.

What do you know about stress? What does it do to you? Most people think all stress is bad. That's not true. There is good stress, and there is bad stress. Here's an example of each:

Meet John and Jane. John has a new job. He likes it very much. He's learning new things every day. Does this cause stress? Yes. But it's good stress.

Jane is working, too. She's working very hard, but she's having problems. Her boss doesn't like her. Does she like her job? No. She hates it. This is causing stress, and it is bad stress.

Bad stress usually affects our personality in negative ways. It often changes us. Optimists become pessimists. Organized people become disorganized. Patient people become impatient. People with bad stress are often angry and tired. They look and feel unhappy. Sometimes they don't think clearly; they forget important things and remember unimportant details. Bad stress is a bad thing.

There are many ways to relieve bad stress. For example, do you get enough sleep and exercise every day? I hope so. We need sleep and exercise. Do you have free time every day? This is also important. You need free time for relaxation. Sleep, exercise, and free time make our lives less stressful.

Do you have questions? No? Okay, then. That's it for today. Remember—I am preparing a short test for you. That's for . . . yes . . . for tomorrow. And your paper is due next Tuesday. And your class project is due next Wednesday. Enjoy your stress-free day!

---

threat = danger. *optimist* = a hopeful person; a person who expects the best.
pessimist = a person who expects the worst. *relieve* = reduce or lessen.

Grammar in Action

Think About Grammar

A. Complete these sentences from Professor Larson's lecture.

1. Today we **are** _____ a new topic.

2. The world **is** _____ very fast.

3. I **am** _____ a short test for you.

Look at the words you wrote. These are the main verbs. The main verbs in these

sentences end with the same three letters. What are they? _____

Look at the **boldfaced** words. These are the auxiliary verbs. What are the auxiliary

verbs in these sentences? _____ _____

_____

B. Complete these sentences from the lecture.

1. He _____ it very much.

2. She _____ it.

3. It often _____ us.

4. They _____ important things.

5. I _____ so.

6. We _____ sleep and exercise.

7. You _____ free time for relaxation.

Some of the verbs end in -s. Write those verbs here. _____

_____ _____

Circle the subjects that go with this -s ending.

    I   You   He   She   It   We   They

Simple Present Tense; Adverbs of Frequency

Introductory Task: What Kind of Personality Do You Have?

A. Try this test.

Write this sentence: **I am a student.**

_____

Compare your handwriting to the samples below. Does it look more like the sample

in a, b, or c? _____

Handwriting sample		Slope	
a.	*I am a student.*	Backward slope	\
b.	*I am a student.*	Forward slope	/
c.	*I am a student.*	Upward slope		

B. Graphologists study handwriting. Sometimes they study the "slope" of the handwriting. They believe handwriting shows a person's personality. Look at this chart.

Handwriting Personality Chart	
Slope	**Personality**
Backward slope: \	You are shy and quiet. You usually think first and speak later. You don't often show your feelings.
Forward slope: /	You are confident and outgoing. You speak openly. You rarely hide your feelings.
Upward slope: |	You are in between. You sometimes feel shy, and you are sometimes very outgoing.

1. Look at your handwriting. Think about the chart. Do the graphologists describe your personality correctly? Circle your answer.

   Yes, they do.   No, they don't.

 2. Discuss as a class: Do you believe the graphologists?

🌐 See the *Grammar Links* Website for more about handwriting and personality.

Simple Present Tense I

FORM

A. Affirmative Statements

SUBJECT	VERB
I	
You	**work.**
We	**match.**
They	
He	
She	**works.**
It	**matches.**

B. Negative Statements

SUBJECT	*DO NOT/DOES NOT*	BASE VERB
I		
You	**do not**	
We	**don't**	**work.**
They		**match.**
He		
She	**does not**	
It	**doesn't**	

(See Appendix 1 for the simple present tense of *be*.)

FUNCTION

A. Habits and Routines

The simple present describes **habits** and **routines**.

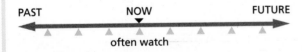

We often **watch** the news on TV.

She **takes** swimming lessons.

B. General Truths

The simple present describes **things that are generally or always true.**

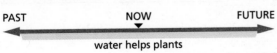

Water **helps** plants grow.

Scientists **study** the natural world.

1. Spelling rules for third person singular (*he, she, it*) simple present verbs:

   - Most verbs: verb + -*s*.

     work → **works**, play → **plays**

   - Verbs ending in -*ch*, -*s*, -*sh*, -*x*, or -*z*: verb + -*es*.

     catch → **catches**, wash → **washes**

   - Verbs ending in consonant + -*y*: Change -*y* to -*ies*.

     study → **studies**, carry → **carries**

   - Some irregular verbs.

     go → **goes**, do → **does**, have → **has**

2. Remember! Use -*s*/-*es* only for third person singular.

   Jane like**s** her new dress.
     NOT: Jane ~~like~~ her new dress.

   I like my new dress.
     NOT: I ~~likes~~ my new dress.

(See Appendix 2 for pronunciation rules for the simple present tense.)

GRAMMAR PRACTICE 1

Simple Present Tense I

✓ **1** **Affirmative Statements:** The Right Job

   A. Certain personalities seem right for certain jobs.

   Line A: Complete the first statement with *be*. Complete the second statement with the simple present of the verb in parentheses.

   Line B: Match the jobs in the box with each personality type. Write a sentence with *be*.

✓an artist	a mechanic	✓a race car driver	✓teachers
✓a comedian	a nurse	✓a scientist	

   1. A. He __is__ very curious. He __researches__ new facts and information.
      (research)

      B. __He is a scientist.__ ✓

   2. A. We __are__ patient. We __explain__ things gently again and again.
      (explain)

      B. __We are teachers.__ ✓

   3. A. You __are__ funny. You __make__ people laugh.
      (make)

      B. __You are a comedian__

4. A. He ___is___ adventurous. He ___enjoy___ (enjoy) danger.

   B. He is a race car driver

5. A. You ___are___ creative. You ___paint___ (paint) beautiful pictures.

   B. You are an artist

6. A. I ___am___ good with my hands. I ___fix___ (fix) cars and trucks.

   B. I am a mechanic

7. A. My sister ___is___ very kind. She ___stay___ (stay) all night with sick people.

   B. My sister is a nurse

B. What is a good job for you? Why? What type of personality do you have? Write the name of the job. Use the jobs in Part A or your own ideas. Then write about your personality. Follow the example.

Example: **JOB:** _manager_

I'm outgoing. I like people.

JOB: _____

1. I _____ .   I _____ .

2. I _____ .   I _____ .

3. I _____ .   I _____ .

See the *Grammar Links* Website for a test to help you find the right job for your personality.

2 Verb Endings: More About Personalities

Write sentences about people with different types of personality.

1. outgoing
   a. This person/have many friends
      This person has many friends.
   b. He/speak openly to people
      He speaks openly to people.

2. organized
   a. This person/have good organizational skills
      This person has good organizational skills
   b. She/use time wisely
      She uses time wisely

3. impatient
   a. This man/hurry all the time
      This man hurries all the time
   b. He/rush around
      He rushs around

4. self-centered   a. This boy/try to get attention

This boy trys to get attention

b. He/think about himself

He thinks about himself

5. pessimistic   a. This girl/worry a lot

This girl worrys a lot

b. She/expect problems

She expects problems

6. obedient   a. This person/follow rules

This person follows rules

b. He/obey the law

He obeys the law

3 Negative Statements: Graphology

Try some graphology. Study the handwriting and statements in Column A. Then write statements about the personality types and handwriting in Column B.

A

Grammar is interesting!

1. **outgoing**

  a. These letters slope forward.

  b. This person is outgoing.

B

Grammar is interesting!

shy

These letters don't slope forward.

This person isn't outgoing. She's shy.

Grammar   is   interesting !

2. **organized**

  a. I leave big spaces between words.

  b. I'm organized.

Grammar is interesting!

disorganized

_____

I'm not _____ . I'm _____.

Grammar is interesting!

3. **impatient**

  a. These words jump up and down.

  b. This person is impatient.

Grammar is interesting!

patient

_____

This person _____.

He's _____.

Grammar is interesting!

4. **pessimistic**

  a. Their lines slope downward.

  b. They are pessimistic.

Grammar is interesting!

optimistic

_____

_____

_____

4 Affirmative and Negative Statements: Graphology—Fact or Fiction?

Complete the passage. Use the simple present tense.

Graphologists _study_ handwriting. They _are match_ a
        1 (study)   2 (match)

person's personality with his or her writing. But this _doesn't work_
                                                   3 (not / work)

for everybody.

For one thing, people's personalities _is not_ always the same.
                                   4 (not / be)

My friend Kim always _write_ with a backward slope, and graphologists
                    5 (write)

tell her she is shy. But Kim _is not_ always shy. In class,
   6 (tell)   7 (not / be)

she _sits_ quietly and she _doesn't ask_ questions.
     8 (sit)   9 (not / ask)

She _watchs_ her classmates and _trys_ to understand
        10 (watch)   11 (try)

the teacher. But Kim also _goes_ to a lot of parties, and at parties, she
                  12 (go)

not has the same personality. She _dances_ a
   13 (not / have)   14 (dance)

lot, and she _tells_ funny jokes! Kim _is_ actually very
        15 (tell)   16 (be)

outgoing and not shy at all!

GRAMMAR BRIEFING 2

Simple Present Tense II

FORM

A. Yes/No Questions and Short Answers

QUESTIONS			SHORT ANSWERS					
DO/DOES	SUBJECT	BASE VERB	YES			NO		
Do	I		Yes,	I		No,	I	
	you			you	do.		you	do not.
	we			we			we	don't.
	they	work?		they			they	
Does	he			he			he	does not.
	she			she	does.		she	doesn't.
	it			it			it	

(continued on next page)

B. *Wh-* Questions and Answers

Wh- Questions About the Subject

QUESTIONS			ANSWERS
WH- WORD	VERB + *-S/-ES*		
Who	**eats**	fish?	I do.
What	**matches**	these shoes?	Your new dress matches them.

Other Wh- Questions

QUESTIONS				ANSWERS
WH- WORD	*DO/DOES*	SUBJECT	BASE VERB	
Who/Whom*	**do**	you	**see?**	Professor Larson.
What	**do**	they	**want?**	Some soup.
Where	**does**	he	**live?**	He lives on Main Street.
When	**does**	it	**snow** here?	It usually snows in November.
How often	**do**	you	**eat** fish?	Two or three times a week.

Whom is more formal than *who*.

GRAMMAR PRACTICE 2

Simple Present Tense II

5 **Short Answers:** You're the Expert!

What are the habits of people with these personalities? Write short answers.

1. shy   Do we speak openly? _No, we don't._

2. disorganized Do these people have poor organizational skills? yes, They are

3. patient   Does she hurry and rush a lot? No, she doesn't

4. quiet   Does he try to get attention? No, he doesn't

5. friendly   Do they like other people? yes, They do

6. generous   Do you share your things with other people? yes, you do

7. honest   Do I tell the truth? yes, I do

6 Yes/No Questions and Answers: The Right Job for Jack

A. Jack Carter is very unhappy at his job. He needs help. Complete the conversation. Change each statement in parentheses to a *yes/no* question, and write short answers.

Jane: Hello, Mr. Carter. My name is Jane Mooney. I'm your career counselor.

_Do you have a problem_____?
<u>1 (You have a problem.)</u>

Jack: Yes, _I do_____. I don't like my job! I really need a new job.
2

Jane: Okay, but I need some information about you.

Do you like meeting new people_____?
<u>3 (You like meeting new people.)</u>

Jack: No, ___I don't_____. I prefer time alone or with my family.
4

Jane: Do you enjoy working with numbers_____?
<u>5 (You enjoy working with numbers.)</u>

Jack: No, __I don't enjoy____! I'm not good with numbers! I always make mistakes.
6

Jane: Okay. Well, that's important, then! __Do you like the outdoors____?
<u>7 (You like the outdoors.)</u>

Jack: Yes, __I do_____. I love the peace and quiet of the countryside.
8

Jane: I see. That's also very important information. Just a few more questions.

Do you like works_____?
<u>9 (Your wife works.)</u>

Jack: Yes, __I do_____.
10

Jane: Does she likes her job_____?
<u>11 (She likes her job.)</u>

Jack: No, __She doesn't_____. She is too busy.
12

Jane: Do you have children_____?
<u>13 (You have children.)</u>

Jack: Yes, __I do_____. We have two children.
14

Jane: _Do they go to school_ ?
15 (They go to school.)

Jack: No, _they don't_ . They finished school, and now they work.
16

Jane: By the way, Jack. What is your job now?

Jack: I work for a large company in New York City. I meet a lot of people, and I work with

numbers all the time. You see, I really need a new job!

B. Discuss as a class: Does Jack's job fit his personality? Why or why not? What is a good job for Jack?

7 *Wh*- **Questions:** An Interesting Job

Learn more about career counselors. Read the answers. Write the questions.
Use the words given.

1. Q: _Where do you find career counselors_ ?
(Where / you / find / career counselors)

   A: In many places.

2. Q: _Who do_ ?
(Who / hire / them)

   A: Employment offices often hire them. Sometimes colleges and universities hire them, too.

3. Q: _what do they their job_ ?
(What / be / their job)

   A: They help people match their personality with good jobs.

4. Q: _Who do you ask them for help_ ?
(Who / ask / them for help)

   A: All kinds of people. Young people and old people. People without jobs and people

   with good jobs.

5. Q: _when do people go to career counslers_ ?
(When / people / go to career counselors)

   A: They go to career counselors when they need a job or when they don't like their job.

6. Q: _How often do career counselors really_ ?
(How often / career counselors / really help people)

   A: They help people quite often.

7. Q: Career counseling sounds interesting. I want to be a career counselor.

   what do I do ?
(What / I / do)

   A: You need to go to school.

what I nree to do

what do I do

8. Q: ___What do I study_____ ?
       (What / I study)

   A: Many things, including psychology.

9. Q: ___What dis Psychology._____ ?
       (What / be / psychology)

   A: Psychology is the study of personalities.

Adverbs of Frequency with the Simple Present Tense

FORM

A. Adverbs of Frequency with *Be*

Adverbs of frequency usually come **after** *be*.	She **is usually** outgoing.
	They **aren't often** here.
	Jane and Dick **are always** happy.

B. Adverbs of Frequency with Other Verbs

Adverbs of frequency usually come **before** other verbs.	Kim **frequently goes** to parties.
	We **sometimes go** together.

FUNCTION

Telling How Often

Adverbs of frequency tell **how often** something happens:

100% of the time

always
almost always
usually
often, frequently
sometimes, occasionally
rarely, seldom
hardly ever
never

0% of the time

1. *Rarely*, *seldom*, *hardly ever*, and *never* are already negative. Don't use *not* with these words.

    We **rarely** go shopping alone.
      NOT: We ~~don't~~ rarely go shopping alone.

    We **never** eat alone.
      NOT: We ~~don't~~ never eat alone.

2. *Ever* means "at any time." Use it in questions and in the phrase *hardly ever*.

    Do you **ever** eat meat?

    We **hardly ever** eat meat.

GRAMMAR PRACTICE 3

Adverbs of Frequency with the Simple Present Tense

8 **The Meaning of Adverbs of Frequency:** Surprise Personality!

A. Some people's personalities don't match their jobs. Kim is at a party. She is talking to a famous Hollywood actor, George Giantmuscle. She gets quite a surprise. Read the conversation.

George at Work

George at Parties

Kim: Excuse me, but aren't you . . . ?

George: Uh . . . yeah. George Giantmuscle. Hi.

Kim: Oh, I don't believe it! I'm so happy to meet you. I watch your movies all the time!

George: Really?

Kim: Yes. I love the movie with the wild horse on Fifth Avenue. How did you ride that horse?

George: Oh, that's my stuntman. I don't ride horses. I don't like big animals.

Kim: Oh, I see. Hmm . . . Well, do you go to a lot of parties?

George: Some, but only with my mother. She goes to a lot of parties, and she occasionally

          takes me with her.

Kim: You're so famous. I bet you meet new people all the time.

George: Yes, I often meet people, but I don't often have time to make friends. I work all the time.

Kim: Ah. Um . . . Well, do you ever dance?

George: Not very often. I'm not very athletic. Maybe I'm just shy. Oh, here comes my mother.

          Time to go. Goodbye.

B. Look again at the conversation in Part A. How often do these things happen?
Circle the correct adverb of frequency.

1. Kim watches George's movies.	(Always)	Often	Sometimes	Seldom	Never
2. George rides horses.	Always	Often	Sometimes	Seldom	Never
3. George goes to parties with his mother.	Always	Often	Sometimes	Seldom	Never
4. His mother goes to parties.	Always	Often	Sometimes	Seldom	Never
5. George meets new people.	Always	Often	Sometimes	Seldom	Never
6. He makes friends.	Always	Often	Sometimes	Seldom	Never
7. He works.	Always	Often	Sometimes	Seldom	Never
8. He dances.	Always	Often	Sometimes	Seldom	Never

C. What surprises you about George, the actor? Write two sentences. Use an adverb
of frequency in each sentence.

1. _He seldom makes friends._ _____

2. _____

3. _____

9 Adverbs of Frequency: My Friend George

Now Kim is telling her friend about George Giantmuscle. Listen to the conversation and write the verbs and adverbs you hear.

Kim: Rosa, _do_ ___1___ you _ever_ ___2___ watch George Giantmuscle videos?

Rosa: ___3___. I ___4___ usually ___5___ out to movies. He's that big tough guy, right?

Kim: Right. You ___6___ him on television.

Rosa: Uh-huh. He ___7___ onto the stage, and everyone screams.

Kim: Well, I know him. We're friends.

Rosa: No! Why ___8___ you ___9___ all the luck? I ___10___ famous people.

Kim: Well, of course not. Famous people ___11___ all their time in the library, and you ___12___ there!

10 Adverbs of Frequency: More About George

Complete the conversation with the words in parentheses. Put the adverbs in the correct place.

Rosa: Well, what's George Giantmuscle like?

Kim: Guess what! He's really shy. He _is usually_
 1 (be / usually) at work, so he _has hardly ever_
 2 (have / hardly ever) time for friends. His mother _take_
 3 (take / sometimes) him to parties.

Rosa: That's amazing. He _____
 4 (be / always) so adventurous and confident in his movies.

Kim: Well, people _____
 5 (surprise / sometimes) you.

Rosa: Hmmm. I wonder. Does he have a girlfriend?

Kim: Forget it, Rosa. He _____
 6 (have / never) time for friends!

11 Adverbs of Frequency: More About You

 Work as a class or in small groups. Do this exercise quickly! Take turns asking one another questions with *Do you ever . . . ?* Answer with adverbs of frequency.

Example: Student 1: Jan, do you ever go to the library?
Student 2: No, I hardly ever go to the library. Pedro, do you ever fall asleep in class?
Student 3: I occasionally fall asleep in class. Mimi, . . .

| Never | Hardly ever | Rarely Seldom | Sometimes Occasionally | Often Frequently | Usually | Almost always | Always |

0%   100%

go to the library	go horseback riding	study all night
fall asleep in class	tell jokes	rush all day
go to the movies	forget people's names	watch the sunset
go to parties alone	forget your telephone number	cry at movies
worry a lot	send letters from a computer	jog before class

12 Simple Present and Adverbs of Frequency: Your Dream Job

 Write a paragraph about your dream job. Talk about what you usually, always, sometimes, etc., do at this job. Use the simple present tense and adverbs of frequency.

 See the *Grammar Link*s Website for a complete model paragraph for this assignment.

Example: I work in a plant nursery. This is my dream job. I usually work five days a week. . . .

Check your progress! Go to the Self-Test for Chapter 1 on the *Grammar Links* Website.

Present Progressive Tense

Introductory Task: Pessimists and Optimists

A. Chip and Chuck are taking a vacation. Read their postcards.

Dear Dan and Eve,

How's it going back in sunny California? We're doing okay. Our ski instructor is trying hard with me, but I'm not learning very fast! At the moment, we're sitting in a cafe. It's **snowing** hard outside, and the wind is blowing. The radio **is playing** some terrible country and western music. Some of the people in our group **are telling** bad jokes. Others **are singing** loudly! We'll be home next Friday. I'm counting the days!

Love,

Chuck

Dan and Eve Stoddard
560 Elm Street
Los Angeles, CA 90065

Dear Dan and Eve,

We're having a great time in Colorado! We **'re learning** a lot about skiing, and we're making some good friends. Right now, we're sitting in a cozy cafe near the ski slopes. The snow **is falling** in big, beautiful flakes outside, and lively music **is playing** in the background. We **'re telling** funny jokes and singing. I'm not thinking about work or school or anything! It's a good life.

Love,

Chip

Dan and Eve Stoddard
560 Elm Street
Los Angeles, CA 90065

---

country and western music = music from the southern and western parts of the United States. *cozy* = comfortable and warm. *lively* = full of energy.

B. Chip and Chuck have different personalities. One is an optimist: He always sees the good side of life. The other is a pessimist: He always sees the bad side. Who is the pessimist? Who is the optimist? How do you know? Copy the sentences from the postcards. Use the **boldfaced** verbs.

I know that _____ is the pessimist because he says:

1. About skiing: _I'm not learning very fast._ _____

2. About the snow: _____

   _____

3. About the music: _____

   _____

4. About the jokes: _____

   _____

I know that _____ is the optimist because he says:

1. About skiing: _____

   _____

2. About the snow: _____

   _____

3. About the music: _____

   _____

4. About the jokes: _____

   _____

Present Progressive Tense I

FUNCTION

A. Actions Happening at the Moment

The present progressive (also called present continuous) describes **actions happening at the moment of speaking**. These actions are often **temporary**. Common time words and expressions used with this meaning of the present progressive include *now*, *right now*, and *at the moment*.

I **am writing** postcards right now.

Snow **is falling**.

PAST   NOW   FUTURE

am writing right now

B. Actions Happening over a Longer Time

The present progressive describes **actions happening over a longer period of time**. These actions are also often **temporary**. Common time words and expressions used with this meaning of the present progressive include *these days*, *this year*, *this semester*, *this week*, *today*, and *this afternoon*.

We **are staying** in a hotel this week.

They **aren't skiing** this afternoon.

PAST   NOW   FUTURE

this week

are staying

Present Progressive Tense I

1 Present Progressive Meanings: Learning to Be an Optimist

Read the letter. Underline the present progressive verbs. Write *N* (for "now") above present progressive verbs that describe what is happening right now. Write *L* above verbs that describe what is happening over a longer period of time.

Dear Mom and Dad,

Guess what! This semester, I'm learning to be a better athlete. I'm taking classes with Dr. Sydney Bennett. He's a very famous psychologist. Dr. Bennett is writing a book called "Optimism for Athletes." He's working with other psychologists here. They are teaching special mental and physical exercises to athletes. They believe these exercises make people optimistic. It's incredible! All their athletes are becoming champions!

Right now, I'm sitting outside the classroom. I'm waiting for Dr. Bennett. And I'm writing this letter. I'm also practicing some of Dr. Bennett's techniques. I'm relaxing my shoulders, but I'm sitting up straight. I'm breathing deeply. I'm thinking happy thoughts. In fact, I'm thinking about you guys! Are you having a good week? Are you relaxing and enjoying yourselves? Or are you working too much, as usual?

Well, Dr. Bennett is coming now. I miss you. Write soon.

Love,

Kurt —the optimist and future Olympic champion!

Present Progressive Tense II

FORM

A. Affirmative Statements		
SUBJECT	*BE*	BASE VERB + *-ING*
I	am / 'm	working.
You / We / They	are / 're	working.
He / She / It	is / 's	

B. Negative Statements		
SUBJECT	*BE + NOT*	BASE VERB + *-ING*
I	am not / 'm not	working.
You	are not	
We	're not	
They	aren't	
He	is not	
She	's not	
It	isn't	

(See Appendix 3 for the spelling rules for *-ing* verb forms.)

Present Progressive Tense II

2   Affirmative Statements: Optimists Win!

Complete the sentences with the present progressive of the verbs in parentheses.
Use full forms, not contractions.

Chip and Chuck __are taking__ skiing lessons right now. Poor Chuck __is doing__ badly.
       1 (take)   2 (do)

But maybe that's because he __is skiing__ like a pessimist! He __is expecting__ to fall, so
                          3 (ski)   4 (expect)

his legs __are shaking__ and he __is losing__ his balance. But Chip __is using__
        5 (shake)   6 (lose)   7 (use)

his body like an optimist. He __is enjoying__ himself, and he __is skiing__ confidently.
                                  8 (enjoy)   9 (ski)

His arms and legs __are working__ together. He __is using__ his mind and body.
                  10 (work)   11 (use)

His mind __saying__ to his body: "Relax! Enjoy! Be positive!"
            12 (say)

3 Affirmative Statements with Contractions: Learning to Win

Kirk is helping a friend play tennis. Complete their conversation with the present progressive of the verbs in parentheses. Use contractions ('m, 's, or 're).

Kirk: Look at me. What am I doing?

Friend: You __'re staring_____ at the ball.
                1 (stare)

Kirk: Good. Now, breathe deeply.

Friend: I am. I __'m breathing_____ deeply and slowly.
                    2 (breathe)

Kirk: Good. Now think about the present.

Friend: Okay. I __'m thinking_____ about the present moment.
                    3 (think)

Kirk: Are you relaxing your muscles?

Friend: Yes. I __'m relaxing_____ my muscles.
                  4 (relax)

Kirk: Okay. Now look at the other player over there. She __'s resting_____
                                                                    5 (rest)

          between shots. Why? Because she . . .

Friend: I know. She __'s saving_____ energy.
                        6 (save)

Kirk: Energy. That's important. And those players always miss the ball, but what are

          they doing?

Friend: They __'re smiling_____ at their mistakes.
                    7 (smile)

Kirk: Right. Are you smiling? Good. And what are you expecting?

Friend: I __'m expecting_____ a perfect shot.
                8 (expect)

Kirk: That's it. Now you __'re acting_____ like an optimist . . . and
                                  9 (act)

          a winner.

4 | Negative Statements with Contractions: Optimistic Tennis

Use the words in parentheses to make negative sentences. Use contractions (*'m not, 're not/aren't, 's not/isn't*).

1. They're thinking about the present moment.

   They're not thinking about the future. OR They aren't thinking about the future.
   (not / think about the future)

2. They're staring at the ball.

   _____
   (not / look at each other)

3. She's expecting a perfect shot.

   _____
   (not / worry about her shot)

4. I'm breathing deeply and slowly.

   _____
   (not / breathe fast)

5. You're smiling at your mistakes.

   _____
   (not / get angry)

6. I'm resting between shots.

   _____
   (not / waste energy)

7. We're acting like optimists.

   _____
   (not / act like pessimists)

See the *Grammar Links* Website for more information about psychology and sports.

5 | Writing Sentences: The Good Side

A. These situations are stressful, but maybe they have a good side. Write a sentence about the good side of each situation. Use the present progressive.

1. Your car isn't working, so you walk to school.

   I'm getting good exercise.

2. Ali's teacher is giving him a lot of homework.

   She is getting a good enoliys

3. Bob is jogging, and it's snowing now.

   Her is

4. Our neighbors are playing loud music next door.

   they will getting in travel

5. You're spending this weekend alone.

   I'm getting a good time for myself

6. Carolyn is dieting, and it's very difficult!

   she is verry

7. I'm not going out much these days.

   _____

8. We're waiting for a plane, and it's three hours late.

   _____

9. Dr. Bauer's students are finding a lot of stress in their lives.

   _____

B. Share your sentences with the rest of the class. Discuss: Who is the most optimistic? Why?

Present Progressive Tense III

FORM

A. *Yes/No* Questions and Short Answers

QUESTIONS			SHORT ANSWERS*					
BE	SUBJECT	BASE VERB + *-ING*	*YES*			*NO*		
Am	I		Yes,	I	**am.**	No,	I	**am not.**
	you							**'m not.**
Are	we			you			you	**are not.**
	they	**working?**		we	**are.**		we	**'re not.**
	he			they			they	**aren't.**
Is	she			he			he	**is not.**
	it			she	**is.**		she	**'s not.**
				it			it	**isn't.**

*Use contractions only in negative short answers, not in affirmative short answers.

(continued on next page)

B. *Wh-* Questions and Answers

Wh- Questions About the Subject

QUESTIONS			ANSWERS
WH- WORD	BE	BASE VERB + -*ING*	
Who	is 's	working?	Chuck is.
What	is 's	happening?	Not much!

Other *Wh-* Questions

QUESTIONS					ANSWERS
WH- WORD	BE	SUBJECT	BASE VERB + -*ING*		
Who/Whom	is 's	Chuck	calling?		He's calling his friend.
What	am	I	eating?		Fish.
Where	are	you	going?		I'm going to the bank.
How	are	they	doing	today?	Great!

GRAMMAR PRACTICE 3

Present Progressive Tense III

6   *Yes/No* **Questions and Answers:** I'm Changing My Life!

Read the conversation. Complete the *yes/no* questions and write short answers.
Use contractions in negative short answers.

Lizzy: So tell me about this new book. <u>Are you reading</u> it now?
           1 (you / read)

Kathy: Yes, <u>I am</u>. It's called *Teach Yourself Optimism*. It's great.
         2

Lizzy: Oh, I have a book like that. It's called *Optimism for Athletes*.
<u>Are we talking</u> about the same book?
      3 (we / talk)

Kathy: No, <u>we don't</u>. At least, I don't think so.
      4

Lizzy: Well, <u>It's helping</u> you?
      5 (it / help)

Kathy: Yes, <u>It is</u>! It's giving me confidence.
      6

Lizzy: <u>They are a lot of people buying</u> this book?
      7 (a lot of people / buy)

Kathy: Yes, <u>they are</u>. It's a bestseller.
      8

Lizzy: Kathy, look out the window! Is that Bob? __he is jogging__ in the snow?
9 (he / jog)

Kathy: Yes, that's Bob. He's reading the book, too. It's really helping him. He's exercising and

dieting and . . .

Lizzy: Kathy, look over there, at that table. That's Carolyn! __She is eating__
10 (she / eat)

pizza for lunch?

Kathy: No, __she doesn't__ . She's eating salad. She's reading the book, too.
11

She's dieting and feeling very positive about it.

Lizzy: I'm exercising and dieting, too. But it's not doing any good.

Look! __I'm getting__ thinner?
12 (I / get)

Kathy: Oh, Lizzy. You're not overweight.

Lizzy: Yes, I am. I'm fat, and I'm getting fatter.

Kathy: Lizzy, you're talking like a pessimist! You really need this book!

7 Wh- Questions: Report the Conversation

Complete the questions with the present progressive.

1. Q: Who is talking to Lizzy? A: Kathy is talking to Lizzy.

2. Q: Where __are they sitting?__ A: They are sitting in a restaurant.

3. Q: What __are they talking about?__ A: They're talking about a new book

4. Q: What _____ A: The book is helping Kathy.

5. Q: Who(m) __is helping Kathy?__ A: The book is helping Kathy, Bob, and Carolyn.

6. Q: Where __is bob jogging?__ A: Bob is jogging in the snow.

7. Q: What __is carolyn eating?__ A: Carolyn is eating salad.

8. Q: How __is she feeling about her diet?__ A: She's feeling very positive about her diet.

9. Q: How __is Lizzy feeling?__ A: Lizzy is feeling pessimistic.

10. Q: What __is she complaining about?__ A: She is complaining about her diet.

11. Q: What __is Kathy saying?__ A: Kathy is saying, "You need the book!"

	WRITING	SPEAKING
1. Use contractions of *wh-* words + *is* in speaking and informal writing.	Who's eating with us tonight?	Who's eating with us tonight?
2. Use contractions of *wh-* words + *are* or *am* only in speaking.	Who **are** you inviting?	Who**'re** you inviting?
	What **am** I doing here?	What**'m** I doing here?

8 **Contractions and Full Forms:** The Help Yourself Show

A psychologist is speaking on a TV talk show. Listen to the interview, and write the full forms of the words you hear.

Interviewer: Dr. Bauer, thank you for coming on the Help Yourself Show. <u>How are</u>
———————————————————
   1

you doing? ————————————————— happening at your clinic these days?
       2

Dr. Bauer: Well, you know, I'm teaching people about stress.

Interviewer: And ————————————————— you doing that?
       3

Dr. Bauer: Positive visualization.

Interviewer: Positive what?

Dr. Bauer: Visualization. Making pictures with our minds. For example, think about this. You and I

are waiting for an important job interview. ————————————————— you doing?
                4

————————————————— you feeling?
     5

Interviewer: My hands are shaking. I'm worrying about the interview.

Dr. Bauer: Right, and that's not helping you. Now. _____ I doing?
              6

             I'm visualizing. I'm making a picture in my mind. _____ this
              7

             picture taking me? Into the interview room. _____ I seeing?
              8

             The interview is going well. The interviewer is smiling and saying, "You're perfect for

             this job." That's positive visualization.

Interviewer: Wow! So _____ coming to your clinic?
              9

Dr. Bauer: People. Lots of people. I'm helping people every day.

9 | Present Progressive: Positive Visualization

Imagine a stressful situation. Use a situation from the box or think of your own situation. Visualize a positive picture about this situation. What is happening? Write a paragraph about this picture. Use the present progressive.

Possible Situations	
the dentist office	learning to ski
the TOEFL exam	your first week in a new country
a long international plane flight	your first date with a new person
an operation in a hospital	a job or college interview
your first day of class	

Example: The Dentist's Office
           I'm sitting in a comfortable chair. I'm listening to soft music on the radio.
           Am I worrying? No, I'm not. . . .

 See the *Grammar Links* Website for a complete model paragraph for this assignment.

Check your progress! Go to the Self-Test for Chapter 2 on the *Grammar Links* Website.

My first day of class.
I'm stending in the enter door.
I'm sitting next to the mexican girL.
I'm listening to the teacher but I don't know what he is saying.
I'm asking what he is saying
I'm very lost. I'm was spiting with the girl next to mi

Simple Present and Present Progressive

Introductory Task: Changes

A. Many things change our personality and habits—sometimes only for a few hours; sometimes forever.

Read about the changes in these people. Underline the **boldfaced** verbs that describe their usual habits and routines. Circle the **boldfaced** verbs that describe what is happening to them now.

1. Yoko **is** usually very sociable. She **goes** to a lot of parties and makes friends

   quickly. But this month she is acting very quiet. She**'s losing** her confidence.

   (Why? This is her first month in a new country. It's stressful.)

2. Carolyn and I almost always **work** very fast and **have** lots of energy. These days,

   we**'re working** slowly, and we**'re making** mistakes. (Why? Our diet **is making**

   us tired. We **aren't eating** right.)

3. You often **act** nervous and tired. But right now you **are acting** quiet and calm.

   (Why? You**'re listening** to relaxing music right now.)

4. Greg **is** usually very organized. He **concentrates** well and **does** a lot in a short

   time. Right now, he**'s trying** to work, but he **is not concentrating**. (Why? It's late

   at night, and Greg is a "morning person." He works better in the morning.)

B. Look at the verbs you circled and underlined in Part A. Then read the statements below and check the correct box.

1. The **boldfaced** verbs that describe usual habits or routines are in the
   ❏ simple present tense.   ❏ present progressive tense.

2. The **boldfaced** verbs that talk about what is happening now, this month, or these days are in the
   ❏ simple present tense.   ❏ present progressive tense.

Simple Present Versus Present Progressive

FUNCTION

A. Simple Present

1. The simple present describes **habits**, **routines**, and things that are generally true.

They **get up** at 7:30. (routine)

Stress **makes** us tired. (generally true)

2. Adverbs of frequency (see Chapter 1) often occur with the simple present.

They **usually** get up at 7:30.

3. Other time expressions also occur with the simple present. They include *every day*, *in the afternoon*, *at night*, *most of the time*, and *on Saturdays* (or other days).

They get up at 9:00 **on Saturdays**.

B. Present Progressive

1. The present progressive describes **temporary actions** happening at the moment of speaking or over a longer period of time in the present.

Shh! He**'s concentrating**. (moment of speaking)

We**'re working** slowly these days. (longer time)

2. Time expressions often occur with the present progressive. They include *these days*, *(right) now*, *today*, *tonight*, *this week*, *this semester*, *this month* and *this year*.

Right now, she's working.
We're living at home **this year**.

Simple Present Versus Present Progressive

1 **Simple Present Versus Present Progressive:** What Changes Personality?

Circle the correct verb form in the sentences.

1. a. Food (gives / is giving) people energy.

   b. But Tom and I (diet / are dieting) this week.

   c. Today we (try / are trying) to eat very little food, but it is difficult.

2. a. Color sometimes (changes / is changing) our personality.

   b. Psychologists say that bright colors often (make / are making) people active and nervous.

   c. For that reason, libraries and hospitals (don't usually paint / aren't usually painting) their walls red.

3. a. Alice (wears / is wearing) a blue dress right now.

   b. She likes blue. It always (makes / is making) her feel calm and relaxed.

4. a. People often (act / are acting) differently in new situations.

   b. For example, Yoko (lives / is living) in a new country this month.

   c. She (acts / is acting) quiet and shy these days.

5. a. I sometimes (get / am getting) tired when the weather is hot.

   b. I (get / am getting) very tired today. It is very hot and hazy.

6. a. Psychologists generally (try / are trying) to help people with personality problems.

   b. They sometimes (help / are helping) people change their personalities and behavior.

7. a. Relaxation (saves / is saving) energy.

   b. It (helps / is helping) people feel positive.

   c. Listen to your breathing. Look at your hands. (Do you relax / Are you relaxing) right now?

2 **Simple Present and Present Progressive:** A New Situation

A. Yoko usually has a routine. But today she is doing something different. Complete the sentences about Yoko. Use the simple present and the present progressive.

USUALLY		TODAY
Eat breakfast with her family	8:00 a.m.	Skip breakfast
Walk to the office	8:45	Catch the fast train downtown
Meet with clients all morning	9:00–12:00	Sit quietly at a desk
Go home for lunch	12:15 p.m.	Buy lunch in the school cafeteria
Answer letters and phone calls	1:00	Go to a laboratory and listen to tapes
See her friends after work	5:00	Go home
Go out in the evening	7:30	Work at her computer

1. Yoko usually _eats breakfast with her family_ .

   Today _she is skipping breakfast_ .

2. It's 8:45. She usually _____ .

   At the moment, _____ .

3. She usually _____ all morning.

   This morning _____ .

4. _____ for lunch.

   Today _____ .

5. In the afternoon, _____ .

   This afternoon _____ .

6. It's 5:10 now. She usually _____ at this time of day.

   Today _____ .

7. Most of the time, she _____ .

   This evening _____ .

 B. What is Yoko doing now? Why is her routine changing? What do you think?
Discuss as a class. Do you all agree?

3 | Simple Present and Present Progressive: There and Here

A. What do you usually do on vacation, at home, with friends, or at work? What are you
doing here today? Write a paragraph about the differences. Use the simple present
and the present progressive. Use the verbs in the box or use verbs of your own.

drink	go	read	visit
eat	live	speak	watch
enjoy	play	study	wear

Example: I usually take a vacation every summer. I visit my parents in China.
This summer, however, I'm not taking a vacation. . . .

See the *Grammar Links* Website for a complete model paragraph for this assignment.

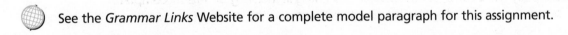 **B.** Exchange papers with a partner. Read your partner's paragraph. Share three ideas
about your partner with the class.

Example: On vacation, my partner often wears shorts. She's not wearing shorts now.
She's wearing a skirt.

Verbs with Stative Meaning

FORM and FUNCTION

A. Overview

Some verbs have stative (not active) meanings. Verbs with stative meaning describe states, not actions. Some common verbs with stative meaning are:

IDEAS	ATTITUDES	EMOTIONS	POSSESSIONS	SENSES	DESCRIPTIONS
forget	need	hate	have	hear	be
know	want	like	owe	see	cost
remember		love	own	smell	look
think				sound	seem
understand				taste	weigh

B. Simple Present Tense for Verbs with Stative Meaning

We usually use the **simple present** with verbs with stative meaning. We rarely use the progressive.

You **seem** nervous at the moment.
NOT: You ~~are seeming~~ nervous at the moment.

C. Verbs with Both Stative and Active Meanings

Some verbs have both a stative and an active meaning. When they have an active meaning, they can be in the progressive.

Stative meaning: Arnold **looks** happy.
 (He seems happy.)

Active meaning: He **is looking** at his mother.
 (He is watching his mother.)

Stative meaning: I **think** he's wonderful.
 (In my opinion, he's wonderful.)

Active meaning: I **am thinking** about Arnold.
 (My mind is focusing on him.)

1. Use the simple present with *have* when it means "own" or "possess."	I **have** a car. **NOT**: I ~~am having~~ a car. She **has** a lot of free time. **NOT**: She ~~is having~~ a lot of free time.
2. In certain special expressions, you can use the progressive with *have*: *have a good time, have trouble, have a problem, have dinner.*	Frank **is having a good time** tonight. He is enjoying himself. Gloria **is having trouble** with her car.

GRAMMAR PRACTICE 2

Verbs with Stative Meaning

4 **Stative and Active Meaning:** Life with Gloria

A. Read the passage. Circle the verbs with stative meaning.

Gloria Jones (is) very tired tonight. Her eyes (are) heavy, and she (is) yawning. Gloria (needs) sleep. Gloria's pillow (feels) soft and comfortable. The music on her radio sounds soothing. The cool air from the open window smells fresh. Gloria (has) a perfect place to sleep! But she isn't sleeping tonight. She (is) thinking about her problems.

B. Circle the correct form of the verbs in parentheses.

Gloria (wants / is wanting) help with her problems. She is writing a letter to

1

Miss Know-It-All. Miss Know-It-All (has / is having) an advice column in the local

2

newspaper. This (is / is being) Gloria's letter.

3

Dear Miss Know-It-All:

Help! I (have / am having) some problems, and I

4

(don't know / am not knowing) what to do. I

5

(need / am needing) some advice. I (think / am thinking)

6 7

you can help me.

First of all, my job (is / is being) a problem. These days,

8

I am working all the time. I usually (love / am loving) my job,

9

but, this is too much!

I also (have / am having) no appetite these days. Food

10

(doesn't look / isn't looking) good to me, and most food

11

(doesn't smell / isn't smelling) and (doesn't taste / isn't tasting)

12 13

so great, either. So I (don't eat / am not eating) these days, and

14

I (lose / am losing) weight.

15

I (think / am thinking) about going to a doctor, but that

16

(costs / is costing) a lot and I (am / am being) too busy. So

17 18

I hope you can help me instead. Please answer this letter.

What is my problem? What is your advice?

Wasting away in Washington,

Gloria Jones

Gloria Jones

C. Complete the letter. Use the simple present or present progressive of the verbs in parentheses.

Dear Miss Know-It-All:

We __want__ (1 (want)) your advice. We _____ (2 (have)) a dear friend named Gloria. She _____ (3 (be)) usually a happy and outgoing person, and we _____ (4 (like)) her very much! But Gloria's personality _____ (5 (change)). She _____ (6 (seem)) angry and nervous these days. She often _____ (7 (forget)) important meetings, and she always _____ (8 (have)) too many things to do. Gloria never _____ (9 (have)) time for her friends. She never _____ (10 (remember)) to call us! These days, Gloria _____ (11 (not / eat)), and she _____ (12 (not / sleep)) well, either. We are worried about her. We _____ (13 (not / understand)) Gloria. Can you help us? We _____ (14 (know)) you give good advice.

Worried in Washington,

Gloria's friends

---

5 | **Simple Present or Present Progressive:** Excuse Me?

Work with a partner. Complete the telephone conversation. Use the simple present or the present progressive of the verbs in parentheses.

1. Teenager: Mom, the phone's for you. It's Billy.

   Mom: Hello, Billy! __Are you having__ (a (you / have)) a good time in Florida?

   Billy: Great! But __I don't have__ (b (I / not have)) any money. I need $300.

2. Student 1: This homework is so difficult!

   Student 2: _____ (a (you / think)) about it too much! Just relax. It's easy!

   Student 1: Really? _____ (b (you / think)) it's easy?

3. Mr. Jones: Jack? This is Mr. Jones from the manager's office. _____ at

     a (I / look)

     your sales report right now.

     Jack: Oh, hi, Mr. Jones. _____ okay?

     b (it / look)

     Mr. Jones: Yes, pretty good!

4. Man: We have a nice new sports car on sale.

     Woman: _____ about the cost. What about a used car?

     a (I / think)

     Man: Sorry. _____ the used cars are all sold.

     b (I / think)

5. Woman: My cat is sick. _____ terrible. She needs an

     a (She / look)

     appointment with the doctor today.

     Receptionist: _____ at the appointment book right now. Is two o'clock okay?

     b (I / look)

6   Editing: A's and B's

Read about personality types. Draw a line through the incorrect **boldfaced** verbs. Write
the correct verb form above the line. There are six incorrect verbs. The first correction is
done for you.

                                                                    divide
Different people **have** different reactions to stress. Medical scientists usually **are dividing**
                  1   2

these reactions into two groups: Type A and Type B. Type A people always **feel** a lot of
                                                                        3

pressure from stress. Type B people **are** more patient and relaxed.
                          4

Frank is a Type A person. He **is having** a new job. There **is being** a lot of stress at his
                                      5   6
job. What is he doing about it? He **is seeming** angry all the time. He **is fighting** with his
                                    7   8
new boss. Joyce is a Type B person. Sometimes she **is hearing** her neighbors' loud music at
                                                  9
night. In fact, this **is happening** tonight. What is she doing about it? She **is listening** to
                    10   11
relaxing music through her earphones. Type B personalities almost always **are reacting** to
                                                                        12
stress in a calm way. Type A personalities usually **have** trouble with stress.
                                                  13

 See the *Grammar Links* Website for more information about Type A and Type B
personalities.

---

7 | **Simple Present and Present Progressive:** Your Personality Type

Which personality type do you think you are, A or B? Why? Write a paragraph. Use the
simple present and present progressive.

Example: I think I have a Type A personality. I worry a lot. I'm worrying right now
about my grammar test tomorrow. . . .

See the *Grammar Links* Website for a complete model paragraph for this exercise.

---

8 | **Stative and Active Meanings:** Personal Profiles

A.

PERSONAL PROFILE QUESTIONNAIRE

1. What causes you the most stress? (Check one)

   ❏ Meeting new people   ❏ Not getting exercise

   ❏ Waiting (in lines, at doctor's offices,   ❏ Moving to a new home
     for late friends, etc.)

   ❏ Not having free time   ❏ Not having money

   ❏ Preparing for a vacation   ❏ Work

                                           ❏ School

See the *Grammar Links* Website for more information about stress.

2. What happens to you when you have stress? What happens to your health? How do you look? How do you feel? Write three sentences. Use verbs with stative meaning. Use the words in the box or use your own ideas.

angry	grouchy	out of sorts	sad	sore
anxious	nervous	pale	sick	tired
exhausted	out of control	restless	sleepless	unhappy

Note: Are any of the words and expressions above new to you? Find them in your dictionary.

When I have too much stress:

My neck is tight and sore.

I look pale and tired.

a. _____

b. _____

c. _____

3. What do you do to relieve stress? Write three sentences about your habits and routines. Use the simple present tense.

I take a warm bath.

I go for a long walk.

a. _____

b. _____

c. _____

 **B.** Share your answers with a partner. Do you have any of the same answers? Share these answers with the class. Which answer is the most common for each question?

Check your progress! Go to the Self-Test for Chapter 3 on the *Grammar Links* Website.

Wrap-up Activities

1 Letter Home: EDITING

Correct the errors in this e-mail message. There are 12 errors with simple present, present progressive, and adverbs of frequency. The first error is corrected for you.

To: lrbrocopp@aol.com
From: Amy_Brocopp@smcvt.edu
Subj: Hello from school

Dear Mom and Dad,

How are you? Thank you for the photos. They are beautiful, and you
     seem
all ~~are seeming~~ fine. Little Maria is looking so tall now!

I miss you, but I am having a great time at school. We are having a good

grammar teacher. She is nice, but she give us a lot of homework. And she

doesn't never finish class on time. I sitting in grammar class at the

moment. The teacher is talking, and I fall asleep. You ask often me: "You

are okay?" The answer is: Yes, I'm. I'm eating in the school cafeteria

these days. I like the pizza! I am thinking it tastes good, and it don't cost

too much.

Goodbye for now. I love you all.

Amy

2 Me or Not Me? WRITING/SPEAKING

Match the paper with the person.

Step 1 On a piece of paper, write three statements about yourself and your personality. Use at least one present progressive verb and one simple present verb. Try to use a verb with stative meaning.

Step 2 Work in a team of four or five. Put your papers together in a bag.

Step 3 Student A: Take a paper from the bag and read the statements aloud. Ask questions to match the paper with the person. That person then becomes Student A.

Step 4 Continue until all students have a turn and all people and papers have a match.

Example statements on paper: I never go to parties.
                       I'm living in a dormitory right now.
                       I love dogs.

Possible questions: Who never goes to parties?
                  Jorge, are you living in a dormitory right now?
                  Do you love dogs?

3 Advertisements: WRITING/SPEAKING

Work in teams of three or four. Write an advertisement for a product that helps with stress or personality problems.

Step 1 Use one idea from Box 1, one idea from Box 2, and one idea from Box 3.

Step 2 Write the advertisement. Add your own description. (For example, how does it look? What is the price? How does it taste, feel, or smell? What does it do?) Use the simple present and the present progressive.

Step 3 Share your advertisement with the rest of the class.

Example:

DO YOU FEEL NERVOUS AND ANGRY THESE DAYS?
The Mind Massager is helping millions of people. People are relaxing and enjoying life.

This wonderful little radio weighs only 50 grams. It goes inside your hat and plays soft music. It sounds wonderful!

Box 1

The Problem

Do you drink coffee every day?
Do you smoke more than 10 cigarettes a day?
Are you a pessimist?
✓ Do you feel nervous and angry these days?
Are you afraid of your boss?

Box 2

Benefits/Changes

Save smokers' lives every day!
✓ Relaxing!
Teach people to be strong!
Tastes better than coffee!
Teach people positive thinking!

Box 3

The Product

No-Smoke Sticks
Strong Guy Secrets (a book)
✓ Mind Massager
"I'm a Winner" self-help tapes
Chunky Chocolate

4 **Where Are You Going?** WRITING/SPEAKING

Step 1 Look at this picture by the famous American artist Norman Rockwell. Write a paragraph about the picture. Describe the people in the picture. Why are they together? What are they doing? What are they thinking about? Use the simple present and the present progressive.

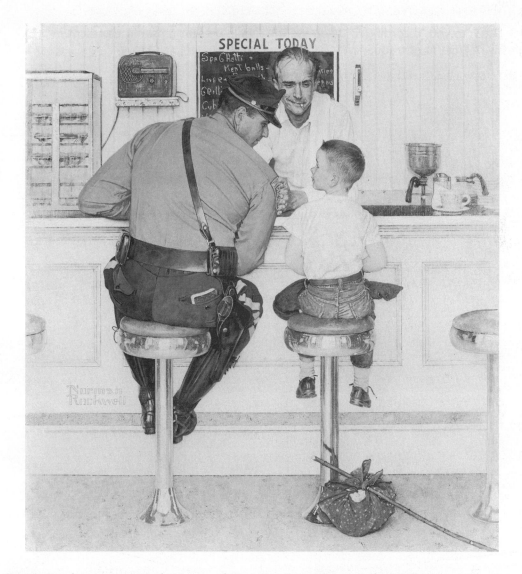

Step 2 Read your paragraph to your classmates. Compare your descriptions.

Example: This is a picture of a policeman and a little boy. They are in a restaurant. The policeman is talking to the little boy. . . .

 See the *Grammar Links* Website for a complete model paragraph for this activity.

Go to the *Grammar Links* Website to see more Norman Rockwell paintings.

More About You: SPEAKING/LISTENING

Step 1 Prepare a short talk about your best friend. Why is this person your best friend? What do you usually do together? What is your friend (probably) doing today?

Step 2 Give your talk in class. Bring along a photo if you can. If possible, tape-record your talk.

Step 3 Listen to your recording. Did you use the simple present tense? The present progressive? Adverbs of frequency?

Past Time

TOPIC FOCUS
Unsolved Mysteries

UNIT OBJECTIVES

the simple past tense
(He *lived* a long time ago. He *wrote* about mysteries.)

used to
(He *used to* travel a lot, but he doesn't travel now.)

the past progressive tense
(The sun *was shining* that morning.)

choosing between the simple past and the past progressive
(They *were standing* on the beach. Suddenly, they *saw* a ship.)

the simple past and the past progressive with *while* and *when*
(She *was talking while* I *was cooking. When* the phone *rang*, I *answered* it.)

Grammar in Action

🎧 Reading and Listening: Unsolved Mysteries

Read and listen.

1   People love stories about ancient history—stories from thousands of years ago. Many of these stories are mysteries. We have a lot of questions about them. Are they all true? What really **happened** to the people and places in these stories?

2   For example, Plato **was** a Greek philosopher. He **lived** and **died** more than 2,000 years ago. He **described** a beautiful continent in the Atlantic Ocean. Plato **called** this continent Atlantis. The Atlantean people were fighting a war with Greece when a terrible earthquake **destroyed** the continent. Atlantis **went** down to the bottom of the sea forever.

3   Was Plato telling the truth when he **wrote** about Atlantis? In ancient times, historians **were** not very scientific. They sometimes used to write from opinion and imagination; but the mystery of Atlantis did not end with Plato.

4   In the middle of the twentieth century, two modern Atlantis stories **became** famous. In one story, the Atlanteans **worked** with the ancient Egyptians. They **helped** the Egyptians build their pyramids. In another story, Atlantis **had** a big magnetic solar crystal. The Atlanteans used this crystal for energy. When the earthquake happened, the crystal **fell** into the ocean, into an area called "The Bermuda Triangle." Thousands of years later, in modern times, many ships and airplanes **disappeared** in this area. Did the magnetic crystal destroy them?

Big Magnetic Solar Crystal

5   Did Atlantis really exist? Who **built** the pyramids? What happened in the Bermuda Triangle? We don't know the answers to these questions. All these stories are unsolved mysteries.

🌐 See the *Grammar Links* Website for more information about Atlantis, the pyramids, and the Bermuda Triangle.

Think About Grammar

A. The simple past tense forms of these verbs are **boldfaced** in the passage. Find them and write them below.

Regular Forms		Irregular Forms	
happen	_happened_	be (is)	_was_
live	_____	go	_____
die	_____	write	_____
describe	_____	be (are)	_____
call	_____	become	_____
destroy	_____	have	_____
work	_____	fall	_____
help	_____	build	_____
disappear	_____		

All **regular** simple past verbs end with the same two letters. What are they? _____

B. Complete this sentence from the passage (paragraph 2).

The Atlantean people ___were___ ___fighthing___ a war with Greece
                                          action 1

when a terrible earthquake ___destroyed___ the continent.
                                action 2

Circle the correct answer.

Action 1 started _____ action 2.

(a.) before

b. after

c. at the same time as

Simple Past Tense; *Used To*

Introductory Task: The Curse of King Tutankhamen

A. Read and listen. Underline all the **regular** simple past tense verb forms.

King Tutankhamen was a boy king in ancient Egypt.

He died in 1323 BC. His people buried him in a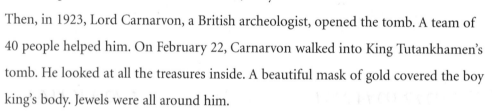
large stone tomb. Some people say the Egyptians
wrote a terrible warning—a curse—on his tomb.
The warning said, "Open this tomb and die!"
No one opened the tomb for more than 3,000 years.
Then, in 1923, Lord Carnarvon, a British archeologist, opened the tomb. A team of
40 people helped him. On February 22, Carnarvon walked into King Tutankhamen's
tomb. He looked at all the treasures inside. A beautiful mask of gold covered the boy
king's body. Jewels were all around him.

A few weeks later, a mosquito bite killed Lord Carnarvon in Egypt. In England,
his dog fell down dead on the same day. In the next seven years, 22 other men from
Carnarvon's team died mysteriously!

More recently, in 1972, a plane carried King Tutankhamen's treasures out of
Egypt. Soon after that, the pilot and engineer had heart attacks and died.

The ancient Egyptians wanted to protect King Tutankhamen's tomb. Did their
terrible curse end the lives of all these people?

> *tomb* = a place to bury people who have died. *archeologist* = a person who finds and
> studies things from the ancient world. *treasures* = very valuable things. *mask* = a cover
> that shows the shape of the body.

B. According to some people, the curse on King Tutankhamen's tomb said, "Open this
tomb and die!" Discuss as a class: Do you believe the curse? Did it come true?

Simple Past Tense I

FORM

A. Regular and Irregular Verbs

1. All **regular** past tense verbs end in *-ed*.
   (See Appendix 4 for spelling rules for the simple past tense.)

   work → work**ed**, live → liv**ed**, study → studi**ed**, wait → wait**ed**

2. The *-ed* ending is pronounced /t/, /d/, or /ɪd/.
   (See Appendix 5 for pronunciation rules for the simple past tense.)

   work/**t**/, live/**d**/, wait/**ɪd**/

3. Many common verbs have **irregular** simple past forms.
   (See Appendix 6 for a list of irregular verb forms. See Appendix 7 for the simple past tense of *be*.)

   have → **had**, go → **went**, do, → **did**

B. Affirmative Statements

SUBJECT	VERB	
I		
You		
He		
She	**lived**	there.
It	**went**	away.
We		
They		

C. Negative Statements

SUBJECT	*DID NOT*	BASE VERB	
I			
You			
He			
She	**did not**	**live**	there.
It	**didn't**	**go**	away.
We			
They			

FUNCTION

Past Actions and States

1. The simple past describes actions and states that began and ended at some time or during some period in the past:

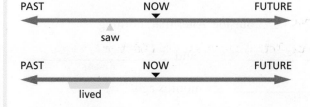

   I **saw** her last night.

   He **lived** a long time ago.

2. Common time expressions used with the simple past include *yesterday*, (*two days*) *ago*, *this* (*morning*), *last* (*night*), *for* (*three years*), *at* (*two o'clock*), and *on* (*Thursday*).

   We worked **for three hours**.

   He died **on Saturday**.

Simple Past Tense I

1 Pronunciation: Tutankhamen's Tomb

A. Listen again to "The Curse of King Tutankhamen" from page 48. Above each verb you underlined, write the sound you hear: /t/ (as in *helped*), /d/ (as in *died*), or /ɪd/ (as in *visited*).

Example:

He di<u>ed</u> in 1323 BC. . . .

B. Read "The Curse of King Tutankhamen" aloud to a partner. Help each other pronounce the past tense verbs correctly.

2 Affirmative Statements (Regular Verbs): The Rest of the Story

Learn more about King Tutankhamen's curse. Complete the stories. Use the simple past tense of the verbs in parentheses.

1. The Soldier's Story (AD 56)

   One morning, my friend and I _visited_ King Tutankhamen's tomb. We
   opened the door and _walked_ inside. A snake
   a (visit)   b (open)   c (walk)
   looked up at us from King Tutankhamen's body. My friend
   d (look)
   killed the snake. But two weeks later, a terrible sandstorm
   e (kill)
   buryed my friend in the desert. He _disappeared_ forever.
   f (bury)   g (disappear)

2. The Farmer's Story (AD 1560)

   I found the tomb many years ago. I was excited, and I _called_ my wife.
                                                          a (call)
   We _wanted_ to go into the tomb. But we _looked_ at the
       b (want)   c (look)
   warning on the tomb, and we _stayed_ outside. After that, nothing
                                 d (stay)
   heppened to us. My wife _lived_ and _worked_
   e (happen)   f (live)   g (work)
   with me for many happy years. She _die_ six months ago.
                                      h (die)

3 Affirmative Statements (Irregular Verbs): Ancient Mysteries

Complete the sentences with the simple past tense of the verbs
in parentheses. Use Appendix 6 and Appendix 7 to help you.

1. The ancient Egyptians _____built_____
   (build)
   the pyramids.

2. These pyramids _____was_____ stone
   (be)
   buildings.

3. They _____had_____ a square base and
   (have)
   four triangle-shaped sides.

   Square = ☐   Triangle = △

4. The Egyptians _____put_____ their kings and queens in the
   (put)
   tombs in the pyramids.

5. They _____left_____ jewels and useful objects next to the kings
   (leave)
   and queens.

6. Other ancient people _____do_____ different things to protect
   (do)
   their dead.

7. For example, they _____ the bodies
   (take)
   to caves.

8. They _____ stories on the walls
   (write)
   of the caves.

9. Many centuries later, Hollywood _____
   (make)
   many movies about ancient mysteries.

10. For example, many people _____ the "Indiana Jones"
    (see)
    and "The Mummy" movies.

11. Indiana Jones _____ a famous scientist.
    (be)
    He _____ to dangerous places with ancient curses.
    (go)

12. The Mummy was a dead body from ancient Egypt. It _____
    (come)
    back to life in the twentieth century and _____
    (become)
    very dangerous.

4 **Regular and Irregular Simple Past:** Time for a Race

A. How many verbs can you think of? Divide into two teams and stand in two lines. The first person in each team writes a **regular** simple past tense verb on the board and runs to the back of the line. The next person writes a different verb. Continue the game until one team can't think of more verbs or for 10 minutes.

B. Now play the game with **irregular** simple past tense verbs.

5 **Negative Statements:** Curse or Common Sense?

Read these warnings. Then look at each picture and write what the people **didn't** do.

WARNINGS:

✔ Give the waiter a good tip!   Pay the rent on time!

Eat right and exercise!   Look right and left before crossing the street!

Stay out of the sun!   Lock the door!

Take a road map!   Confirm the reservation!

1. _She didn't give the waiter a good tip._   2. _____

_____

3. _____   4. _____

_____   _____

5. _____   6. _____
   _____   _____

7. _____   8. _____
   _____   _____

6 Time Expressions with Simple Past: Personal History

Write a paragraph about your past life. Write at least five sentences. Use time expressions (see the examples in the box).

Example: *I came to the United States five years ago.*

| last Tuesday | a long time ago | in 1999 |
| yesterday | this morning | for many years |

See the *Grammar Links* Website for a complete model paragraph for this assignment.

Simple Past Tense II

FORM

A. Yes/No Questions and Short Answers

QUESTIONS			SHORT ANSWERS					
DID	SUBJECT	BASE VERB	*YES*			*NO*		
	I			I			I	
	you			you			you	
	he			he			he	
Did	she	**go?**	Yes,	she	**did.**	No,	she	**didn't.**
	it			it			it	
	we			we			we	
	they			they			they	

B. Wh- Questions and Answers

Wh- Questions About the Subject

QUESTIONS		ANSWERS
WH- WORD	PAST FORM OF VERB	
Who	**went?**	She did.
What	**disappeared?**	The ship disappeared.

Other Wh- Questions

QUESTIONS				ANSWERS
WH- WORD	*DID*	SUBJECT	BASE VERB	
Who(m)	**did**	they	**help?**	They helped their friends.
What	**did**	he	**do?**	He worked.
Where	**did**	you	**go?**	Home.
How	**did**	it	**disappear?**	Very fast.

GRAMMAR PRACTICE 2

Simple Past Tense II

7 **Yes/No Questions and Answers: My Secret Past**

On a piece of paper, write a statement about your past life (you can use one from your paragraph in Exercise 6). Put your papers together in a bag. Take a paper from the bag. Ask *yes/no* questions to match the paper with the person.

Example: Q: Did you come to the United States many years ago?
　　　　　 A: Yes, I did./No, I didn't.

8 **Wh- Questions:** Doctor Fossil, It's a Curse!

Complete the *wh-* questions in the conversation. Use the simple past tense of the verbs in parentheses.

Mrs. Jumpy: Dr. Fossil, please help me. You're a famous archeologist.

And you know all about mysterious curses.

Dr. Fossil: What ___did you say_____,
            1 (you / say)

Mrs. Jumpy? Curses?

Mrs. Jumpy: Yes. Curses. Do you see this old statue? It attacked me

last weekend. And last night it broke my glass table.

Dr. Fossil: _____ you this statue?
            2 (who / give)

Mrs. Jumpy: I bought it in Mexico last week, on my vacation.

Dr. Fossil: I see. So _____ last weekend?
            3 (what / happen)

Mrs. Jumpy: When I opened my closet door, the statue jumped out and hit me!

Dr. Fossil: Mrs. Jumpy, when _____ the statue in the closet?
            4 (you / put)

Mrs. Jumpy: Last Thursday, when I came home. I put the statue and all my suitcases on the shelf.

Dr. Fossil: And how full _____?
            5 (that shelf / be)

Mrs. Jumpy: Oh, very full. It was hard to close the closet door.

Dr. Fossil: Okay. What _____ with the statue after it attacked you?
            6 (you / do)

Mrs. Jumpy: I put it on the glass table in the living room. But last night I heard a terrible crash.

I saw the broken glass and the statue on the living room floor!

Dr. Fossil: Where _____?
            7 (the glass table / be)

Mrs. Jumpy: In front of the window.

Dr. Fossil: Ah. And what else _____?
            8 (you / hear)

Mrs. Jumpy: A terrible noise. A loud wind—like the voice of death. Oh, Doctor!

Dr. Fossil: This is no curse, Mrs. Jumpy. I can help you. First, take the suitcases out of your closet.

Put the statue inside, and close the door. And one more thing: Close your windows on

windy nights!

9 *Yes/No* and *Wh-* **Questions:** The Mystery of the Mayans

A. The Mayans, like the Egyptians, were ancient pyramid builders. Write *yes/no* or *wh-* questions about the Mayans. Use the information given.

1. The ancient Mayans lived in southern Mexico and Guatemala.

   Q: Where did the ancient Mayans live?

   A: In southern Mexico and Guatemala.

2. They lived there from 2000 BC to AD 1542.

   Q: _____

   A: From 2000 BC to AD 1542.

3. They built beautiful pyramids.

   Q: _____

   A: Beautiful pyramids.

4. Workers, noblemen, and priests lived in Mayan society.

   Q: _____

   A: Workers, noblemen, and priests.

5. The workers built the pyramids.

   Q: _____

   A: Yes, they did.

6. The noblemen wrote laws for the people.

   Q: _____

   A: The noblemen.

7. The priests didn't work in the fields.

    Q: _____

    A: No, they didn't. They organized religious services.

8. In 1542, the Mayans disappeared.

    Q: _____

    A: In 1542.

9. They didn't leave any information about their disappearance.

    Q: _____

    A: No, they didn't.

10. The forest buried their beautiful cities and pyramids.

    Q: _____

    A: The forest.

> *noblemen* = people from families with a high social position. *priests* = men who perform religious duties for a society.

B. What is the mystery of the Mayans? Write a question about the mystery. Then share your question with a partner. Do you have the same question?

See the *Grammar Links* Website for more information about the Mayans and their civilization.

Practicar

GRAMMAR BRIEFING 3

Used To

FORM

A. Affirmative Statements

SUBJECT	*USED TO*	BASE VERB	
He			
	used to	live	here.
We			

B. Negative Statements

SUBJECT	*DID NOT*	*USE TO*	BASE VERB	
He	did not			
		use to	live	here.
We	didn't			

C. *Yes/No* Questions and Short Answers

QUESTIONS					SHORT ANSWERS	
DID	SUBJECT	*USE TO*	BASE VERB		YES	NO
Did	we	use to	live	here?	Yes, we **did**.	No, we **didn't**.

(continued on next page)

D. *Wh-* Questions and Answers

Wh- Questions About the Subject

QUESTIONS				ANSWERS
WH- WORD	*USED TO*	BASE VERB		
Who	**used to**	**be**	famous?	Colorado Jones did.
What		**happen**	a lot?	He used to travel.

Other Wh- *Questions*

QUESTIONS					ANSWERS
WH- WORD	*DID*	SUBJECT	*USE TO*	BASE VERB	
What	**did**	he	**use to**	**do?**	Travel.
When		they		**go?**	A long time ago.

FUNCTION

Past Habits and Routines

Used to describes past habits and routines that are no longer true in the present. *Used to* makes it easy to compare the past with the present.

past	present
I **used to** travel a lot, but I **don't travel** anymore.	

GRAMMAR HOT SPOT!

1. Use the base form of *used to* in negative sentences and in questions with *did*.

   I **didn't use to** watch TV.
   NOT: I didn't ~~used~~ to watch TV.

   What **did** you **use** to do?
   NOT: What did you ~~used~~ to do?

2. *Use* is a regular main verb. It has a different meaning from *used to*.

   I **used** your pen.

Used To

10 **Used To**: Changing Lifestyles

Two conversation partners are talking about Jorge's new class. Complete the conversation with the correct forms of *used to* and the verbs in parentheses.

Elizabeth: The students in your class are very interesting. I'm sure they have many stories to tell.

Jorge: That's right. We all __used to live__ in different countries, and we
1 (live)

__didn't use to be__ students. But life is changing for us now. For example, Brigitte
2 (not / be)

__used to work__ in a bookstore in France. Now she wants to be a banker.
3 (work)

Elizabeth: And what __used to do Antonio__? Where
4 (Antonio / do)

__did he use to live__?
5 (he / live)

Jorge: Well, Antonio _____ a banker in Guatemala. Now he wants to
6 (be)

buy a bookstore in New York City!

Elizabeth: Really? And your teacher said something about actors in your class. Who

_____ actors?
7 (be)

Jorge: Mariko and Kenji, from Japan.

Elizabeth: __They use to work__ in Tokyo?
8 (they / work)

Jorge: No. They __didn't use to spend__ much time in Tokyo.
9 (not / spend)

They __use to travel__ around Japan. But now they want to open a
10 (travel)

flower shop in Kyoto.

Elizabeth: And what about you?

Jorge: Well, I __used to teach__ Spanish in Puerto Rico. But now I want to go
11 (teach)

home and teach English.

11 **Used To**: Changes in My Life

A. Write six sentences about changes in your own life. Use *used to*. Write at least three negative sentences. Use verbs from the box or use your own ideas.

be	go	live	talk to
feel	have	see	work

Examples: I used to have a dog, but now I have no pets.
I used to live in a small town, but now I live in a city.

B. Share your sentences with a partner. Ask and answer questions about your past lives.

Examples: A: *What kind of dog did you use to have?* B: *A small brown one.*
A: *Did you use to like the small town?* B: *Yes, I did.*

C. Work in small groups. Find one change that is the same for everyone in your group. Share it with the whole class.

Example: *Our parents used to bring us to school, but now we come alone.*

TALKING THE TALK

		WRITING	SPEAKING
1.	In speaking, contractions of *wh-* words + *did* are common. *Did you* is often pronounced *didja* or *ja*.	Did you see it?	Did**ja** see it?
		When did you go?	When **ja** go?
		What did he do?	What**'d** he do?
		Who did she see?	Who**'d** she see?
2.	In speaking, *used to* is often pronounced *useta*.	He used to travel a lot.	He **useta** travel a lot.

---

12 Contracted Forms: A Changed Man

An archeologist is speaking on a radio talk show. Listen to the interview and write the full forms of the words you hear.

Interviewer: Dr. Colorado Jones! We're happy to have you on our show tonight. Tell us about

your exciting life. You love to explore the secrets of the ancient world, right?

Dr. Jones: Well, I ___used to___ love traveling. But I stopped all that a long time
                                  1

ago. It was a great life. I saw the world. I traveled to pyramids, temples, ancient cities . . .

Interviewer: So _____ travel with?
                          2

Dr. Jones: By myself. Alone. I _____ need company in those days.
                                      3

Interviewer: _____ feel lonely sometimes?
                      4

Dr. Jones: No, I never _____ think about it.
                              5

Interviewer: So what happened? _____ get tired of it?
                                        6

Dr. Jones: No, my wife didn't like it.

Interviewer: Your wife? _____ get married?
                                7

Dr. Jones: About 10 years ago.

Interviewer: And _____ meet her?
                              8

Dr. Jones: In a travel agency! I only _____ two agencies in all my
                                              9

               traveling years, and she _____ work in one of them.
                                            10

Interviewer: So _____ give up all those adventures for love?
                         11

Dr. Jones: No, I didn't give them up. Now I can see the world and have a family life too!

               My father-in-law found the way.

Interviewer: _____ he do?
                    12

Dr. Jones: He bought us a television and a VCR as a wedding gift!

13 Simple Past Tense and *Used To*: Explain This!

Work in small groups. Write a story to explain the picture. Write at least six sentences.
Use the simple past tense and *used to*. Explain these mysteries: Where were these
people? Who was the woman? Why was the man in the box? Did she use to know
him? What happened next?

Example:

See the *Grammar Links* Website for a complete model paragraph for
this assignment.

Check your progress! Go to the Self-Test for
Chapter 4 on the *Grammar Links* Website.

Past Progressive Tense; Simple Past and Past Progressive; Past Time Clauses

Introductory Task: The Flying Dutchman

Read the true story below. Each underlined sentence tells about two actions. Which action started first? Write *1* above the first action and *2* above the second action.

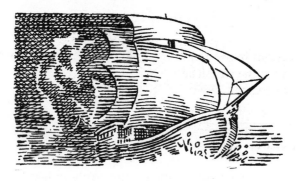

1. In 1580, a Dutch ship was traveling from Holland to Indonesia.

                 2   1
    It disappeared in a storm while it was passing South Africa.

2. A few years later, some sailors met the ship again.

    They were sailing in the Atlantic Ocean when they saw the ship.

3. It was moving fast toward them.

    When the sailors saw this, they tried to send a signal to the ship.

4. While they were shouting and waving, it disappeared.

5. The ghost ship appeared again in the eighteenth and nineteenth centuries.

    When people heard about the ship, they called it "the Flying Dutchman."

---

sailors = people who work on ships. *signal* = message. *ghost* = a dead person who appears again in the world.

 See the *Grammar Links* Website for more information about the Flying Dutchman.

Past Progressive Tense I

FORM

A. Affirmative Statements

SUBJECT	PAST OF *BE*	BASE VERB + *-ING*
I		
He		
She	was	
It		moving.
You		
We	were	
They		

B. Negative Statements

SUBJECT	PAST OF *BE* + *NOT*	BASE VERB + *-ING*
I		
He	was not	
She	wasn't	
It		moving.
You		
We	were not	
They	weren't	

(See Appendix 3 for the spelling rules for *-ing* verb forms.)

FUNCTION

A. Actions in Progress in the Past

The past progressive describes actions **in progress** (not completed) at a specific time in the past. The action started **before** the specific time and might continue **after** the specific time.

The sun **was shining** at six o'clock.

PAST 6:00   NOW   FUTURE

was shining

B. Actions Happening over a Longer Time in the Past

The past progressive also describes actions happening over a longer **period** of time in the past.

I **was studying** last night from six o'clock till midnight.

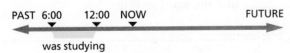

PAST 6:00   12:00   NOW   FUTURE

was studying

Past Progressive Tense I

1 **Affirmative Statements: A Strange Scene**

In March 1939, some people saw the Flying Dutchman again, near a beach in South Africa. Joanna, a South African woman, described the scene. Complete her story with the past progressive of the verbs in parentheses.

At six o'clock, the sun _was shining_ _____. Some children
1 (shine)

__are playing__ in the sand. I __was living__
2 (play)   3 (lie)

in the sun. Then I noticed the people around me. They _____
4 (look)

at the sea. A woman _____ at a ship. The ship
5 (point)

_____ toward the beach. It _____
6 (come)   7 (rain)

hard around the ship. The ship's sails _____ in the wind. It looked
8 (blow)

like the ship _____.
9 (fly)

2 **Affirmative and Negative Statements: What Really Happened?**

Tom and Joanna are trying to remember what they saw on the beach. They don't agree. Complete their conversation with the past progressive of the verbs in parentheses.

Tom: I remember it exactly! I _was swimming_ _____ in the ocean with Kate.
1 (swim)

The ship _wasn't moving_ _____. It was cloudy around the ship, but it
2 (not / move)

_____. One man _____
3 (not / rain)   4 (wave)

at the ship.

Joanna: No, you're wrong! I saw the ship first. You and Kate _____.
5 (not / swim)

Both of you _____ into the sea. The ship
6 (walk)

_____ still. The storm _____
7 (not / stand)   8 (push)

it very fast. That man _____ at the ship. He
9 (not / wave)

_____ you and Kate! But you
10 (call)

_____ attention to him.
11 (not / pay)

Past Progressive Tense II

FORM

A. *Yes/No* Questions and Short Answers

QUESTIONS

PAST OF *BE*	SUBJECT	BASE VERB + *-ING*
Was	I	
	he	
	she	moving?
	it	
Were	you	
	we	
	they	

SHORT ANSWERS

YES			NO		
Yes,	I	was.	No,	I	was not.
	he			he	
	she			she	wasn't.
	it			it	
	you			you	
	we	were.		we	were not.
	they			they	weren't.

B. *Wh-* Questions and Answers

Wh- Questions About the Subject

QUESTIONS

WH- WORD	PAST OF *BE*	BASE VERB + *-ING*
Who	was	moving.
What		

ANSWERS

I was.
The ship was.

Other *Wh-* Questions

QUESTIONS

WH- WORD	PAST OF *BE*	SUBJECT	BASE VERB + *-ING*
What	was	it	doing?
When	were	you	watching?
Where	were	they	going?
How	was	it	moving?

ANSWERS

It was moving.
Yesterday.
Home.
It was moving fast.

Past Progressive Tense II

3 *Yes/No* **Questions and Short Answers:**
The Disappearance of Flight 19

A. At 2:00 p.m. on December 5, 1945,
five U.S. Navy planes (Flight 19) left the
Fort Lauderdale Navy base in Florida.
They never came back. Read this report
from the Navy base captain.

Flight 19 was doing a short training exercise over the Atlantic Ocean.
At first, we were receiving good radio contact with Flight 19. The planes
were flying fast, at 200 miles per hour. Then, at 2:30, the commander of
Flight 19 reported problems. His compass was not working. His radio
was giving him trouble, too. From 3:45 until 4:15, we had no contact.
During that time, our radio officer was trying to make contact, but he
was not getting an answer. He was starting to worry. Finally, at 4:15,
he received this message from the flight commander: "I don't know
our location." The last message, at 4:25, said, "We're in trouble. I think
we are . . ." The commander never finished the message.

compass = an instrument that shows direction.

B. Ask the captain about his report in Part A. Write *yes/no* questions with the words
given. Then read the story again and write short answers.

1. Flight 19/do/a short exercise?

   Q: <u>Was Flight 19 doing a short exercise?</u>

   A: <u>Yes, it was.</u>

2. you/receive/good radio contact at first?

   Q: <u>Were you receiving good radio contact at first?</u>

   A: <u>Yes, we were.</u>

3. the planes/fly/slowly?

   Q: _____

   A: _____

4. the commander's compass/work/at 2:30?

   Q: _____

   A: _____

5. his radio/work/well?

   Q: _____

   A: _____

6. your radio officer/try/to make contact from 3:45 till 4:15?

    Q: _____

    A: _____

7. he/get/an answer?

    Q: _____

    A: _____

8. he/start/to worry?

    Q: _____

    A: _____

4 **Wh- Questions:** The Bermuda Triangle

Flight 19 was flying in the Bermuda Triangle, a dangerous area of the Atlantic Ocean. Christopher Columbus wrote about the Bermuda Triangle in 1492. Read the notes from his journal. Write *wh-* questions about the **boldfaced** words. Use *where, who, what,* or *when.*

1. At that time, I was sailing **west from Europe.**

    Where were you sailing?

2. **My men and I** were looking for a new way to the Indies.

    _____

3. **On October 11,** we were traveling in good weather.

    _____

4. Then we came into a terrible place. **Strange things** were happening.

    _____

5. Bright lights were flashing **in the sky.**

    _____

6. **White water** was bubbling in the sea.

    _____

7. I noticed my compass. The needle **was jumping around.**

    _____

8. I looked at my companion. He was covering **his face** with his hands.

_____

9. The other men were watching **me**. They were waiting for instructions. But I was frightened too.

   who were the men watching?

5 *Wh-* Questions: What Were You Doing?

A. Work with a partner. Take turns asking and answering questions about times in your lives. Use ideas from Columns A and B or use your own ideas.

Example: A: What were you thinking about five minutes ago?
          B: My lunch.

A	B
Where / live?	five minutes ago
What / think about?	last night at midnight
What / do?	last year
Who / teach you?	three years ago
Who / live with?	at 3 o'clock this morning

B. Write the most interesting answer here. Then share it with the class.

Example:

Last year, Ernesto was living on a boat in Florida.

_____

_____

GRAMMAR BRIEFING 3

Simple Past Tense Versus Past Progressive Tense

FUNCTION

A. Simple Past

Use the simple past for actions or states that began and ended in the past. The action or state is **completed**.	I **explained** it to my friend last night. (I finished explaining.)

(continued on next page)

B. Past Progressive

1. Use the past progressive for actions **in progress** (not necessarily completed) in the past.	I **was explaining** it to my friend last night. (Perhaps I didn't finish.)
2. The past progressive often **describes a scene**. It gives **background information** for stories. The simple past gives the **action** of the story.	The sun **was shining**. We **were swimming**. (background description) Suddenly, a strange ship **appeared**. We **swam** back to the beach. (action)

GRAMMAR HOTSPOT!

Use the simple past (not past progressive) for verbs with stative meanings. (See Chapter 3 for more on verbs with stative meaning.)	They **had** a good map. **NOT**: They ~~were having~~ a good map.

GRAMMAR PRACTICE 3

Simple Past Versus Past Progressive Tense

6 **Simple Past Versus Past Progressive:** Mystery in My Living Room

Read the sentences below. Check (✓) the sentences that describe completed actions.

1. Last night, I stayed up late. ___✓___

2. I was watching a murder mystery on TV. _____

3. I watched the movie for about an hour. _____

4. Halfway through the movie, I was falling asleep. _____

5. So I went to bed. _____

6. I closed my eyes and fell asleep. _____

7. Suddenly, big, scary monsters were running after me. _____

8. They were laughing and showing their long teeth. _____

9. I woke up and ran into my parents' bedroom. _____

10. They said, "No more mystery movies for you!" _____

7 Simple Past Versus Past Progressive: A Careful Man

A. Complete the conversation with the simple past or past progressive of the verbs in parentheses.

Jorge: Do you want to hear a joke?

Liz: Okay.

Jorge: Well, one day Christopher Columbus and his men _were sailing_ _____ in the
1 (sail)

Atlantic Ocean. Suddenly, they _noticed_ _____ a small boat in the
2 (notice)

distance. The man in the boat _____ a big basket of fish on top
3 (hold)

of his head! Columbus and his men _____ the man onto their
4 (take)

ship. Then Columbus asked him, "What _____ you

_____ out there?" The man _____:
5 (do)   6 (answer)

"Yesterday morning, I _____ near my island. A big storm
7 (fish)

_____ my boat all the way out here."
8 (push)

"But what about that basket on your head?"

"Oh, I _____ my boat. You see, my boat is very light, and the
9 (help)

basket is very heavy. I _____ the boat to sink. So I
10 (not / want)

_____ to carry the basket myself!"
11 (decide)

B. Work in small groups. Can you explain the joke? What was the man's mistake?
Share your group's explanation with the class.

8 **Simple Past Versus Past Progressive:** Explaining the Mystery of Flight 19

A. Here are some different explanations for the disappearance of Flight 19. Complete the sentences with the verbs from the box. Use the simple past and the past progressive.

1. From the Navy:

be	✓have	hit	disappear	make

Flight 19 _had_ (a) a bad compass. Some of the pilots _were_ (b) new and nervous. On that day, they _were making_ (c) their first sea flight. They probably _hit_ (d) a storm and _disappear_ (e) into the ocean.

2. From the movie *Close Encounters of the Third Kind*:

take	happen	visit

It _happened_ (a) like this. At that time, some aliens from outer space _visiting_ (b) the Atlantic Ocean. Their UFOs _took_ (c) the five planes back to the alien planet.

3. From Charles Berlitz (author of *The Bermuda Triangle*):

fly	pull	wait

At 4:15, Flight 19 _was flying_ (a) over the Bermuda Triangle—right above the lost continent of Atlantis. The magnetic crystal from Atlantis _was waiting_ (b) for them. It quickly _pull_ (c) the planes to the bottom of the sea.

B. What do you think about the mystery of Flight 19? Write at least five sentences. You can agree with one of the explanations in Part A or write your own explanation. Use the simple past and the past progressive.

See the *Grammar Links* Website for a complete model paragraph for this assignment.

9 **Simple Past and Past Progressive:** Story Writing—It Happened One Night

A. In small groups, complete this mystery story. Write background sentences for paragraphs 1 and 2. Write action sentences for paragraphs 3 and 4. Follow the directions in parentheses. Use your imagination!

1   *One night, I was driving along a country road.*

(Add two sentences. Describe the weather: snow? rain? wind? stars? clouds? Example: *It was raining. . .*)

2   *Suddenly, someone jumped out in front of me. He looked strange.* (Add two sentences. Describe the person. What was he wearing? What was he doing?)

3   *The strange person pointed to a house at the side of the road.* (Add three sentences. Use verbs with stative meaning. How did the house **look**? What did you **see**? What did you **hear**?)

(See Grammar Briefing 2 in Chapter 3 and Grammar Briefing 3, Grammar Hotspot! in this chapter to review verbs with stative meaning.)

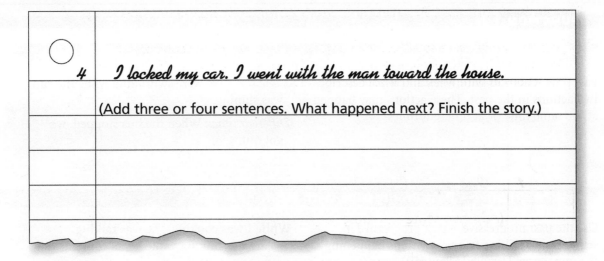

4   *I locked my car. I went with the man toward the house.*

(Add three or four sentences. What happened next? Finish the story.)

B. Share your story with other groups in the class.

Past Time Clauses with *When* and *While*

FORM

A. Sentences with Time Clauses

1. A time clause has a **time expression** (*when, while*), a **subject**, and a **verb**.

time expression	subject	verb
When	**I**	**shouted**

2. A time clause is not a complete sentence. It must be used with a main clause.

   time clause   main clause
   When I shouted, she ran away.
       NOT: ~~When I shouted.~~

3. A time clause can come before or after a main clause. Use a comma (,) after the time clause when the time clause comes **first**.

   time clause   main clause
   When I shouted, she ran away.

   main clause   time clause
   She ran away when I shouted.

B. *When* and *While*

Use the **simple past** in *when* time clauses. Use the **past progressive** in *while* time clauses.

When I **shouted**, she ran away.

While she **was eating**, her taxi came.

(continued on next page)

A. Overview

Past time sentences with *when* and *while* describe two actions in the past. These actions may happen at the same time or at different times.

Same time: We were swimming while the sun was shining.

Different times: When the bus stopped, we got out.

B. Past Progressive + Past Progressive with *While*

Use the past progressive + past progressive in sentences describing two past actions happening at the same time. Use *while* clauses.

While I **was cooking**, she **was talking**.
= She **was talking** while I **was cooking**.

PAST   NOW   FUTURE

was cooking
was talking

C. Simple Past + Simple Past with *When*

Use the simple past + simple past in sentences describing two past actions—one happening immediately after the other. The action in the *when* clause happened first.

When I **shouted**, she **ran** away. = She **ran** away **when** I **shouted**. (First I shouted; then she ran away.)

PAST   NOW   FUTURE

shouted   ran away

D. Past Progressive + Simple Past

The past progressive and the simple past can occur in the same sentence. This means that one action was in progress when the second action interrupted it or happened during it.

While she **was eating**, her taxi **came**.

She **was eating when** her taxi **came**. (First she was eating; then her taxi came.)

PAST   NOW   FUTURE

(taxi) came
was eating

Use *while* + past progressive for the action that started first. Use *when* + simple past for the second action.

Be careful! The *when* + simple past clauses in **C** and **D** above show two different orders of action. With main clauses in the **simple past** (**C**), the *when* clause shows the **first** action. With main clauses in the **past progressive** (**D**), the *when* clause shows the **second action**.

I **left** when the taxi came. (First the taxi came; then I left.)

I **was leaving** when the taxi came. (First I started to leave; then the taxi came.)

GRAMMAR PRACTICE 4

Past Time Clauses with *When* and *While*

10 ***While* Clauses + Past Progressive:** The Way to Go

Last month, Lien and Ida took a trip from Chicago to Denver at the same time. Lien went by train, and Ida went by car. Their trips were very different. Write sentences with *while* and the past progressive. Use the information given.

Lien	**Ida**
1. sit comfortably	drive through heavy traffic

While Lien was sitting comfortably, Ida was driving through heavy traffic.

2. have lunch in the restaurant car	eat at a fast-food restaurant

3. look at the scenery	stare at the road signs

4. read a mystery story	study her road map

5. listen to soft music	listen to the traffic report

6. talk to the other passengers	pump gas

7. walk around the train	worry about her car

8. take a nap	try to stay awake

11 *When* **Clauses + Simple Past:** Money, Money, Money

A. Read the pairs of sentences about some lucky people. Which action happened first?
Write *1* above the first action and *2* above the second action.

1. The bus company paid me a lot of money. A bus hit my car.
   [handwritten: 2 above "paid", 1 above "hit"]

2. Someone left her $100,000. He died.
   [handwritten: 2 above "left", 1 above "died"]

3. My new book came out. It sold 10,000 copies.

4. We won a lot of money in the casinos. We went to Las Vegas.

5. They looked under the floor of their house. They found a box of jewels.

6. She said yes. He asked a rich woman to marry him.

7. They saw a treasure inside. They looked into the cave.

B. Combine the pairs of sentences in Part A. Use the simple past tense. Write the
clauses in the correct order. Add commas where appropriate.

1. When _a bus hit my car, the bus company paid me a lot of money._

2. _Someone left her $100,000,_
   when _He died_

3. When _It sold 10,000 copies_
   _____

4. _____
   when _____

5. When _____

6. When _He asked a rich woman to marry him, she said yes_

7. _They saw a treasure inside_
   when _They looked into the cave_

12 **Simple Past and Past Progressive:** What Happened to Mr. Charles?

A. Read the article. Underline the time clauses.

Where Is Mr. Charles?

Chicago Businessman Disappears Mysteriously

On the morning of July 2, 2004, Mr. Gregory Charles got up very early. He was preparing for an important business meeting in San Francisco. When his wife woke up, he was packing his suitcase. He looked very nervous. While he was eating breakfast, his taxi came. When he got to the station, his train was waiting at the platform. He got on the train from Chicago to San Francisco. When the train arrived in San Francisco, his business client was waiting at the station. But Mr. Charles was not on the train. Later, the police arrested one of the porters on Mr. Charles' train. When they arrested him, he was wearing Mr. Charles' expensive gold watch! The porter said, "I found it while I was checking the bathroom on the train." Mr. Charles' wife is very worried. She has no idea where he is.

platform = place where trains stop for passengers. *arrested* = stopped and took to the police station.

B. Look at the article again. For each of the sentences with time clauses, check the action that **started first.**

1. His wife woke up. He packed his suitcase. ✓

2. He ate some breakfast. His taxi came. ✓

3. He got to the station. His train waited at the platform. ✓

4. The train arrived in San Francisco. His client waited at the station. ✓

5. The police arrested the porter. He wore Mr. Charles' expensive gold watch. ✓

6. I found it. I checked the bathroom on the train. ✓

13 Simple Past and Past Progressive: Mr. Charles' Life Story

The police are looking for Mr. Charles. His life story is very useful to them. Use the information in the file to write sentences with *while* time clauses. Write the clauses in the correct order. Add commas where appropriate.

CHARLES, Gregory, Jr.: History

1. 1975–1996	Lived in Chicago.	1996: Met his future wife.
2. 1996–June 1997	Studied in Germany. May 1997: his father died.	
3. 1997–June 2004	Managed his father's business. May 2003: Borrowed $100,000.	
4. June 10–17 2004	Made a business trip. June 12: Stopped in Las Vegas.	
5. June 12–16 2004	Stayed in Las Vegas. June 13–16: Lost $100,000 in a casino.	
6. June 17, 12–4 p.m.	Flew home to Chicago. 2 p.m.: Called his bank from the airplane.	

1. While _he was living in Chicago, he met his future wife._

2. _His father died_
   while _he was studied in Germany._

3. _He Borrowed $100,000_
   while _Managed his father's business._

4. While _he made a business trip,_
   He stopped in las vegas

5. While _He was stayed in Las vegas,_
   He lost $100,000 in a casino.

6. _He called his bank from the airplane_
   while _He was Flew home to Chicago._

14 *When* and *While* Clauses: What the Porter Said

A. Listen to the interview between the police and the porter from Mr. Charles' train. Match the clauses in A with the clauses in B.

A	B
1. He was sitting alone	_____ a. I saw it there.
2. What was he doing	___1___ b. when I came in to check his ticket
3. He disappeared	_____ c. a different man was sitting there.
4. Was his compartment empty	_____ d. while I was talking to him.
5. When I looked in again	_____ e. I was checking the bathroom.
6. He was staring out the window	_____ f. while you were checking it?
7. When the train stopped in Denver	_____ g. while I was checking the other compartments.
8. While I was cleaning the sink	_____ h. when you checked again?

B. On a sheet of paper, write sentences with the clauses you matched in Part A. Add commas where appropriate.

Example: 1. ___He was sitting alone when I came in to check his ticket.___

15 *When* and *While* Clauses: Solving the Mystery

A. Work in small groups. Examine the police evidence below, the biography in Exercise 13, page 78, and the porter's story in Exercise 14. Discuss: What happened to Mr. Charles?

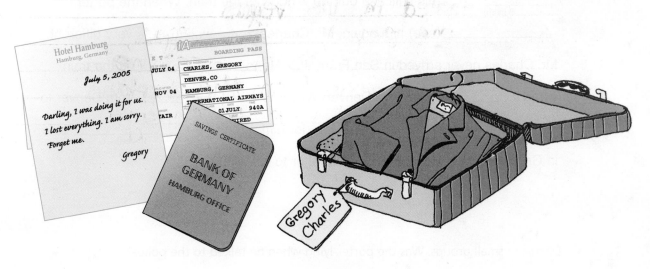

B. Did your group guess the answer to the mystery? Find out. Complete the story below with the simple past or the past progressive of the verbs in parentheses.

Chicago Metropolitan Police

Final Report: Disappearance of Charles, Gregory, Jr.

When Mr. Charles _lost_____ his money in Las Vegas, he
          1 (lose)

_decided_____ to escape. He moved all his money from Chicago to Hamburg,
  2 (decide)

Germany. He _was wearing_____ a business suit when he _got_____ on
        3 (wear)   4 (get)

the train. But he was carrying old clothes in his suitcase.

While the porter _____ the other compartments, Mr. Charles
                  5 (visit)

quickly _____ his clothes in the bathroom and _____ his
        6 (change)   7 (leave)

watch on the sink. When he _____ out of the bathroom, he
                           8 (come)

_____ his suitcase out the window of the train. When the porter
  9 (push)

_____ (see) him again, Mr. Charles _____ very different.
  10 (see)   11 (look)

Mr. Charles never arrived in San Francisco. He _____ off the train
                                 12 (jump)

when it _____ in Denver. While he _____ from Denver to
        13 (arrive)   14 (fly)

Germany, the police _____ for him. When he _____ safe
             15 (look)   16 (feel)

in Germany, he _____ a letter to his wife.
       17 (send)

C. Discuss in small groups: Was the porter lying when he talked to the police?

Check your progress! Go to the Self-Test for
Chapter 5 on the *Grammar Links* Website.

Wrap-up Activities

1 The Mystery of the *Titanic*: EDITING

The *Titanic* was a famous ship that went down in the Atlantic Ocean in 1912. Correct the errors in this research report about the *Titanic*. There are 12 errors with the simple past, the past progressive, and past time clauses. The first error is corrected for you.

History 101

The Mystery of the *Titanic*

When the White Star Line built the *Titanic,* the owners ~~feel~~ *felt* very confident. This was the biggest and strongest ship in the world. But on April 15, 1912, the *Titanic* hit a huge iceberg while it went to America.

Why the *Titanic* went down? The iceberg was very big. The ship was travel fast when the accident happened. But perhaps the "accident" was really something else—a curse!

Nearly 3,000 years ago, a woman dies in ancient Egypt. She was a priestess (a female priest) for the sun god, Amon Ra. Priests and priestesses use to be very important in ancient times. So when she died, the Egyptians cover her body with special bandages. In the twentieth century, people taked the mummy to the British Museum in London. While the museum was showing the mummy, many terrible things happened in the building. After that, the British Museum was giving the mummy to a museum in New York.

On April 15, 1912, the *Titanic* carryed this mysterious mummy passenger to New York. She ~~was~~ disappearing forever in the Atlantic Ocean with 1,500 other passengers. Did she destroyed them? The answer is a mystery.

 See the *Grammar Links* Website for more information about the *Titanic*.

A. Write your own life story. Mention five important dates and events in your life.

Example:

My Life

Dates	Events
1973–1991	Living in Jakarta, Indonesia
1993	Got married

Memory Book

1997–2011	I was living in Guatemala, Rio Dulce.
15, 1997	It's my birthday in Independance day.
2011	I arrived to u.s. from high school.
2015	Whe I got to Las Vegas with the church members.
2015	Whe I Gratuated from high school.

B. Work with a partner. Find out what he or she was doing during the important dates and events in your life.

Example: A: What were you doing while I was living in Jakarta?
B: I was going to college.
A: Where were you living when I got married?
B: In Mexico City.

C. What did you learn about your partner? Write at least five sentences. Use past time clauses with *when* and *while*.

Example: <u>While I was growning up in Jakarta, Marisa was going to college.</u>

<u>(She) was living in Mexico when I got married.</u>

 See the *Grammar Links* Website for a complete model paragraph for this activity.

3 **My Personal Adventure:** WRITING/SPEAKING

A. Write a short story about a strange adventure that happened to you (true or not true). Write at least five sentences. Use time clauses with *when* and *while*, past progressive, and simple past. Answer the questions below to help you.

When did it all happen?

What were you doing when it happened? Where were you living?

What happened first?

What did you do when this happened?

What happened next?

Example: It all began one morning in 1988. When it happened, I was living at my uncle's house.

 See the *Grammar Links* Website for a complete model paragraph for this activity.

B. Share your stories in small groups. Ask one another questions. Find out: Are the stories true?

4 **Make Sense of Nonsense!**: WRITING/SPEAKING

Work in small groups. Explain these strange sentences. Write a story that includes one of the sentences. Write at least four sentences. Use at least one past progressive, one simple past, one time expression, and one time clause with *when* or *while*. Share your story with the class.

The spaghetti disappeared.

She put the fish in her pocket.

We climbed down the telephone pole.

Then they saw the shoe on the bicycle.

Example: Juan invited Olga to dinner last week. He put salad and fish on her plate. But poor Olga hated fish. While Juan was answering the telephone, <u>she put the fish in her pocket.</u> When she left the house, she dropped the fish in the garden.

Future Time

TOPIC FOCUS
Living with Technology

UNIT OBJECTIVES

- ▪ *be going to*
  (It *'s going* to *rain.*)

- ▪ *will*
  (We *will see* many changes in the future.)

- ▪ choosing between *be going to* and *will*

- ▪ the present progressive and the simple present for future time
  (Linda *is flying* to Amsterdam next week. Flight 202 *leaves* at 9:00 tomorrow morning.)

- ▪ future time clauses
  (*When he becomes president,* he is going to work hard.)

- ▪ future and factual conditionals
  (I *will help* you *if you ask me. If you heat water,* it *boils.*)

Grammar in Action

Reading and Listening: Technology in the Twenty First Century

Read and listen.

1   Technology is changing the world we live in and **will continue** to change our lives in the future. What changes **will** technology **bring**?

2   First of all, more and more people **are going to use** the Internet. The Internet is an international network of computers. Right now, many millions of people in hundreds of countries communicate through the Internet. And that number **is going to grow**. Some people say that soon the Internet **is going to connect** all the schools, libraries, businesses, and personal computers in the world. When this happens, we probably **won't need** offices, banks, stores, or schools. We**'ll stay** home and do everything "online," through the Internet. And we **won't need** post offices; we**'ll send** all our letters by electronic mail, or "e-mail."

3   Computer technology **will** also **allow** people to live in a "virtual reality" world. Users of this technology move in an imaginary world. They see and touch virtual objects, and they talk to other people in Internet space. Perhaps, one day, many people **will study** in virtual universities, take virtual vacations, and go to their friends' virtual weddings.

4   Other types of technology **will help** to solve problems. For example, new medical technology **will make** people live longer. They **will work** less; robots, or intelligent machines, **will do** the most difficult and dangerous jobs for them.

5   But technology **will** also **bring** problems. When people live longer, how **are** we **going to find** food for them all? Today, if we need more homes, we build new cities. But if the world's population grows to 9 billion, where **will** everyone **live**? How **will** we **control** our robots if they become too intelligent? **Will** people **spend** too much time on the Internet and forget how to live in the "real" world?

6   Technology brings great hope for this century. But **will** we **learn** to control it before it controls us?

---

network = a group of connections. *virtual reality* = a type of technology that makes computer pictures and sounds seem very real. *imaginary* = not real; in your mind.

Think About Grammar

A. Read the passage again. Look at the **boldfaced** words. Do these words talk

about events in the past, in the present, or in the future? _____

B. Some of the verbs from the passage are in boxes a and b below.
Write the **boldfaced** words that come before these verbs in the passage.

a. (from paragraph 2)   b. (from paragraph 4)

_____	_____	_____ grow		_____ help
_____	_____	_____ connect		_____ make

C. The **boldfaced** words in the passage show two ways of talking about future time.
Write the words that show future time.

a. _____

 _____

b. _____

D. Look at these two sentences from paragraph 5. Circle the correct answers below.

a. Today, if we need more homes, we build new cities.

b. But if the world's population grows to 9 billion, where will everyone live?

 1. Which sentence talks about the future?   a.   b.   a. and b.

 2. Which sentence uses the simple present tense after *if*?   a.   b.   a. and b.

Chapter 6

Expressing Future Time

Introductory Task: Education and Information

A. Professor Larsen is making predictions about education in the future. Read them with a partner. In the *You* column, check (✓) the predictions that you both think will come true.

Presentation 1		
Predictions:	**You**	**Professor Larsen**
1. We are going to see a lot of changes in education.	❏	☑
2. School classrooms will look the same as they do now.	❏	❏
3. Students will do all their class work on computers.	❏	❏
4. Students are going to spend a lot of time at home online.	❏	❏
5. Young children will play in virtual reality kindergartens.	❏	❏
6. Professors will fly to many different countries on the same day.	❏	❏
7. Professors will give tele-lectures through videophones.	❏	❏
8. Some students will become technology addicts.	❏	❏

tele-lectures = lectures on TV. *videophones* = telephones that show video pictures of the speakers. *addict* = someone who needs something in an unhealthy way.

B. Did Professor Larsen make the same predictions as you? Listen to the lecture. In the *Professor Larsen* column in Part A, check (✓) the predictions you hear.

Future Time with *Be Going To* I

FORM

A. Affirmative Statements

SUBJECT	PRESENT OF *BE*	*GOING TO*	BASE VERB
I	am		
	'm		
You			
We	are	going to	change.
	're		
They			
He			
She	is		
	's		
It			

B. Negative Statements

SUBJECT	*BE + NOT*	*GOING TO*	BASE VERB
I	am not		
	'm not		
You	are not		
We	're not	going to	change.
They	aren't		
He	is not		
She	's not		
It	isn't		

FUNCTION

A. Overview

Be going to talks about future events. Common time words and expressions used with *be going to* include *tomorrow, next (weekend), this (evening), in (50 years),* and *soon.*

Tomorrow, Bob**'s going to** see a ball game.

She's **going to** finish **soon**.

B. Predictions and Immediate Expectations

1. *Be going to* makes **predictions** (guesses) about the future.

   Life**'s going to be** different in 50 years.

2. Often, *be going to* talks about the **immediate**, or very near, future. Something happening right now makes us expect something to happen very soon.

   Look out! You**'re going to fall** into that hole.
   (I can see the hole and the danger right now.)

C. Plans

Be going to expresses plans made before the moment of speaking.

A: What's going to happen now?

B: We**'re going to hear** a lecture.
(Someone planned the lecture before now.)

Future Time with *Be Going To* I

1 **Predictions and Future Time Expressions:** Technology and the Future

A. Technology is going to change our lives in many ways. Here are some experts' predictions. Complete the sentences. Use the correct form of *be going to* with the verbs in parentheses.

1. Technology addiction _is going to be_____ an international problem.
   (be)

2. Electronic information _is going to control_ our lives.
   (control)

3. Books and newspapers _is going to disappear_ from everyday life.
   (disappear)

4. Your child _is going to watch_____ about 40 hours of TV each week.
   (watch)

5. We _are going to find_____ intelligent life in space.
   (find)

6. You _are going to take_ virtual reality vacations in space.
   (take)

7. Intelligent machines, or robots, _are going to do_____ all our
   (do)
   dangerous jobs.

8. The twenty-first century robot _it going to think_____ just like a human.
   (think)

9. All college students _are going to study_ computer programming.
   (study)

10. I _am going to meet_ a lot of new friends on the Internet.
    (meet)

See the *Grammar Links* Website for more information about robots of the future.

B. Which predictions in Part A do you believe? When do you think they are going to happen? Write at least five sentences. Use the predictions in Part A or write your own. Add time expressions.

Example: _Everyone in this country is going to have a cell phone soon._____

C. Work with a partner. Compare your predictions. Were they the same? Discuss any
different predictions.

2 **Immediate Expectations:** **What's on TV?**

Bill's new TV has a lot of channels. He is checking them out. What is going to happen
next in these TV programs? Use the words given and write sentences with *be going to*.
Use contractions.

1. He/say, "Marry me!"
   He's going to say, "Marry me!"

2. She/say, "No!"
   She's going to say, "No!"

3. The spaceship/land
   The spaceship is going to land

4. The woman/run away
   The woman is going to run away

5. The short runner/win the race
   The short runner is going to win the race

6. The tall runner/come in second
   the tall runner is going to *be* come in second.

3 Predictions: The Weather Forecast

What does Bill learn from the TV weather channel? Use the words given and write sentences with *be going to*. Use contractions.

1. It/be sunny here in Chicago

   It's going to be sunny here in Chicago.

2. We/have warm temperatures

   we are going to have warm temperatures

3. I/enjoy this beautiful day

   I'm going to enjoy this beautiful day.

4. It/rain in the East

   It's going to rain in the East

5. A storm/move in from the West soon

   A storm is going to move in from the West soon

6. They/need umbrellas in California, too

   They are going to need umbrellas in California, too

4 Making Plans: Get a Life!

These people are technology addicts, but they are planning to change. Read these journal entries about their present habits. Write sentences about things they are going to do differently. Make negative statements. Then use the words in parentheses to make affirmative statements.

Now	Plans For Change
1. I go online every night.	*I'm not going to go online every night.*
	Tonight I'm going to read a good book.
	(read a good book)

Now

2. We talk to friends in a chat room all night.

3. I stay home and work on my computer every weekend.

4. You eat your dinner alone in front of the computer.

5. Your friends worry about you.

6. Paula checks her e-mail many times every afternoon.

7. My children play virtual reality games all weekend.

8. Clara takes her Palm Pilot to class every day.

9. My friend and I read the Internet newsline every day.

Palm Pilot

Plans for Change

2. We are going to talk to friends in a chat room.
Tonight I'm going to do our homework.
(do our homework)

3. I'm going to stay home and work on my computer every weekend.
This weekend I'm going to go for
(go for a long bicycle ride)

4. _____
_____ this evening.
(eat with your family)

5. _____
_____
(see a big change in you)

6. _____
_____ this afternoon.
(turn off the computer)

7. _____
Next weekend _____
(play outside)

8. _____
_____ tomorrow.
(leave it at home)

9. _____
Today _____
(buy a newspaper)

chat = friendly, informal conversation.

Future Time with *Be Going To* II

FORM

A. *Yes/No* Questions and Short Answers

QUESTIONS

PRESENT OF *BE*	SUBJECT	*GOING TO*	BASE VERB
Am	I		
Are	you we they	going to	change?
Is	he she it		

SHORT ANSWERS

YES				NO		
Yes,	I	am.	No,	I	am not. 'm not.
	you we they	are.		you we they	are not. 're not. aren't.
	he she it	is.		he she it	is not. 's not. isn't.

B. *Wh-* Questions and Answers

Wh- Questions About the Subject

QUESTIONS

WH- WORD	PRESENT OF *BE*	*GOING TO*	BASE VERB
Who	is	going to	change?
What			

ANSWERS

My children are.

My life is.

Other *Wh-* Questions

QUESTIONS

WH- WORD	PRESENT OF *BE*	SUBJECT	*GOING TO*	BASE VERB
Who(m)	am	I		meet?
What	is	he	going to	do?
How	are	we		pay?

ANSWERS

The president.

He's going to talk.

With a credit card.

TALKING THE TALK

In speaking, *going to* is often pronounced *gonna*.

WRITING	SPEAKING
They aren't **going to** tell us.	They aren't **gonna** tell us.
What are you **going to** do?	What are you **gonna** do?

Future Time with *Be Going To* II

5 **Yes/No Questions and Short Answers:** Surprise, Surprise!

A. Mrs. Baker is telling her middle-school science class about a surprise for next week. Complete the conversation with *yes/no* questions and short answers. Use *be going to* with the words in parentheses.

Annie: _____Are you going to tell_____ us about the surprise?
1 (you / tell)

Mrs. Baker: Yes, _____. It's about technology.
2

Fred: _____ fun?
3 (it / be)

Mrs. Baker: Yes, _____. Lots of fun.
4

Johnny: _____ us to the video arcade? You know,
5 (you / take)

where they have those great video games?

Mrs. Baker: No, _____.
6

Fred: What? Video games? Wow! _____ free games?
7 (we / get)

Mrs. Baker: No, _____you're not_____, Fred. You didn't hear me!
8

I said, no video games.

Johnny: What about the kids in the ninth grade class?

_____, too?
9 (they / come)

Mrs. Baker: No, _____. Now, wait, everybody!
10

You're not listening. _____ about this,
11 (I / talk)

or _____ all the time? Okay.
12 (you / shout)

We're going to have a visitor from SETI. SETI means "Search for Extraterrestrial

Intelligence." It's a group of people who are looking for life in space. Our visitor is going

to tell you about SETI's project.

Annie: Great! A visitor! _____ us to the video arcade?
13 (he / take)

Mrs. Baker: No, _____. Oh, you kids! You never listen!
14

> *extraterrestrial* = outside the earth.

 See the *Grammar Links* Website for more information about SETI.

B. In groups of four, act out the conversation in Part A. Practice using *gonna* wherever possible.

6 *Wh-* Questions: Life in Space?

The visitor from SETI is talking to Mrs. Baker's class. Read his answers to the students' questions. Write the students' *wh-* questions about the boldfaced words in the answers.

1. Students: _What are you going to talk about today?_

   Visitor: I'm going to talk about **the SETI space project**. SETI is an organization of scientists and other people. We're looking for intelligent life in space.

2. Students: How _are you going to do that_?

   Visitor: We're going to do that **with telescopes and satellites**. We are building a network of high-power radio telescopes and satellites. We're going to watch the sky with them. We're going to study the stars and planets.

3. Students: Where _are the telescopes going to be_?

   Visitor: Our telescopes are going to be **in our backyards**.

4. Students: How many telescopes _are you going to have_?

   Visitor: We're going to have **5,000 telescopes** around the world.

5. Students: Who _is going to pay for this study_?

   Visitor: **We** are going to pay for this study, but we're also going to ask for help.

6. Students: Who _are you going to ask_?

   Visitor: We're going to ask **government agencies** such as NASA, the National Aeronautics and Space Agency.

7. Students: How long _is the project going to last_?

   Visitor: The project's going to last **for many years**, I hope—at least until the middle of this century.

8. Students: What _is going to happen in this century_?

   Visitor: **Many exciting things** are going to happen in this century.

9. Students: What _are you going to find_?

   Visitor: We're going to find **extraterrestrial life**.

10. Students: When _are you going to find it_?

    Visitor: I don't know, exactly, but we're going to find it **one day**. And with our new technology, I believe it's going to happen soon.

7 Yes/No and Wh- Questions: Your Future Projects

 A. Think of your future life and plans. Are computers going to be very important in your life? Work in groups of three or four. Ask and answer questions with *be going to*. Use the ideas below, or make up your own ideas.

Some uses of computers:

online chat rooms

Internet shopping and banking

online interviews

virtual reality vacations

Internet college courses

Internet newslines

Example: A: How are you going to stay in touch with your classmates?

B: I'm going to chat with them online.

C: Are you going to do your shopping on the Internet?

 B. Write a paragraph about your future plans. Write at least six sentences. Use *be going to* and time expressions.

See the *Grammar Links* Website for a complete model paragraph for this assignment.

GRAMMAR BRIEFING 3

Future Time with *Will* I

FORM

A. Affirmative Statements

SUBJECT	WILL	BASE VERB
I		
You		
He	will	
She	'll	change.
It		
We		
They		

B. Negative Statements

SUBJECT	WILL + NOT	BASE VERB
I		
You		
He	will not	
She		change.
It	won't	
We		
They		

(continued on next page)

Predictions

1. Like *be going to*, *will* is used to make predictions (guesses) about things we expect in the future.

My life **will** be different next year.

2. Uncertain predictions often include *maybe*, *probably*, and *I think*.

I will **probably** be smarter in 20 years.

3. Certain predictions often include *(almost) certainly* and *definitely*.

I will **definitely** be older in 20 years.

GRAMMAR HOTSPOT!

1. Remember! Use *will* and the base form of the verb.

He **will leave** tomorrow.
NOT: He will ~~to leave~~ tomorrow.
NOT: He will ~~leaving~~ tomorrow.
NOT: He will ~~leaves~~ tomorrow.

2. In statements, *maybe* and *I think* usually go at the beginning of the sentence. *Probably*, *certainly*, and *definitely* usually go **after** *will* and **before** *won't*.

I think I'll be smarter in 20 years.

I'**ll probably** see you later.

I **probably won't** see you tomorrow.
NOT: I ~~won't probably~~ see you tomorrow.

GRAMMAR PRACTICE 3

Future Time with *Will* I

8 Predictions with *Will*: Robots of the Future

Robots are very "smart" machines. Find out about them. Correct the errors in the **boldfaced** words. Use *will* with the verbs given.

Scientists have great plans for the robots of the future. Maybe one day you **will seeing** [*will see*] a robot that
looks like you. Its "eyes" **will to be** [*will be to*] small cameras. **It maybe will** [*It will maybe*] hear through microphones.
Minicomputers **making** [*will making*] the "brain." This robot **will speaks** through a sound box in its throat, and
it **will have probably** [*will probably have*] soft plastic "skin." It will look like a human, but it **won't certainly be** human!

microphone = an instrument that sends sounds from one place to another.

Future Time with *Will* II

FORM

A. *Yes/No* Questions and Short Answers

WILL	SUBJECT	BASE VERB
QUESTIONS		
Will	I	
	you	
	he	
	she	**change?**
	it	
	we	
	they	

SHORT ANSWERS

YES			NO		
Yes,	I		No,	I	
	you			you	
	he			he	
	she	**will.**		she	**will not.**
	it			it	**won't.**
	we			we	
	they			they	

B. *Wh-* Questions and Answers

Wh- *Questions About the Subject*

QUESTIONS

WH- WORD	WILL	BASE VERB
Who	**will**	**change?**
What		**happen?**

ANSWERS

My children will.
Life will change.

Other Wh- *Questions*

QUESTIONS

WH- WORD	WILL	SUBJECT	BASE VERB
What		it	**do?**
When	**will**	they	**change?**
Where		you	**go?**

ANSWERS

It will change.
Very soon.
Home.

(continued on next page)

More Uses of *Will*

1. Use *will*:

   - To make quick decisions at the moment of speaking. | Are you going? Okay, **I'll go** too.

   - To make promises. | I **will** always **love** you.

   - To make and refuse requests. | A: Will you buy me a computer?
     B: No, I **will not buy** you a computer.

   - To make offers and express willingness. | Wait! Don't carry that heavy box. **I'll help** you.

2. Time expressions with *will* usually come at the beginning or end of the sentence. *Always* and *never* come between *will* and the main verb. | We'll see you **Wednesday**.
   Next year I'll buy you a computer.
   I'll **never** leave you.

GRAMMAR PRACTICE 4

Future Time with *Will* II

9 ***Yes/No* Questions and Short Answers: Smart—or Human?**

A. Will future robots think like humans? What do you think? Write questions with *will* and the words in parentheses. Then write your answers.

1. (future robots/be intelligent)

   Q: Will future robots be intelligent?

   A: Yes, they will./No, they won't.

2. (they/solve math problems)

   Q: Will they solve math problems?

   A: yes, they will.

3. (a future robot/feel happy or sad)

   Q: Will a future robot feel happy or sad?

   A: No, they won't.

4. (it/understand our feelings)

   Q: Will it undersatand our feeling?

   A: yes, they will or No they won't

5. (we/teach robots to remember people's names and faces)

Q: _We'll teach robots to remember people's names and faces?_

A: _Yes, they will._

6. (they/make decisions in new situations)

Q: _Will they make decisions in new situations?_

A: _maybe, they will._

7. (robots/have imaginations)

Q: _Will robots have imaginations._

A: _No, they won't._

B. Work with a partner. Ask each other your questions in Part A. Are your answers the same? Discuss any answers that are different.

TALKING THE TALK

	WRITING	SPEAKING
1. In speaking and writing, pronouns + contractions of *will* (*'ll*) are common. Only in speaking, nouns + *'ll* are also common.	She**'ll arrive** soon.	She**'ll arrive** soon.
	My wife **will arrive** soon.	My wife**'ll arrive** soon.
2. Only in speaking, *wh-* words + *'ll* are common.	What **will** she do?	What**'ll** she **do**?
	When **will** you come?	When**'ll** you **come**?

---

10 **Contractions with *Will*:** Roboroach

Complete the story with *will* and the verbs given. Use the contracted form of *will* with pronouns. Use the full form of *will* with nouns.

In the future, we ___'ll use___ robots everywhere for difficult and dangerous jobs,
1 (use)

in places where you and I ___'ll___ never ___travel___ .
2 (travel)

Right now, for example, the University of Tokyo has a very

useful "pet" robot. It's a cockroach, with an electronic backpack!

Japanese scientists ___will program___ , or teach, this
3 (program)

robot to go through very small spaces. Maybe this "roboroach"

___will go___ into buildings after earthquakes,
4 (go)

or maybe it ___will find___ dangerous land mines after wars. Other,
                5 (find)

human-size robots ___will look___ for lost planes and ships at the bottom
                      6 (look)

of the sea. They ___will take___ photographs on faraway planets in space.
                   7 (take)

They ___will test___ underground mines and nuclear factories for dangerous gases.
        8 (test)

Who knows? Perhaps one day your daughter ___will play___ tennis with a robot
                                              9 (play)

"coach"! Or your son ___will rent___ a robot tutor for private math lessons at home.
                       10 (rent)

> *land mines* = small bombs buried in the ground.

See the *Grammar Links* Website for more information about Roboroach.

11 Contractions with *Will*: Future Robots: Smart—or Human?

A. Listen to the interview with Dr. Weber, an expert in robots of the future. Write the words you hear. After pronouns, write contractions of *will* ('*ll*). After nouns or *wh-* words, write *will*.

Interviewer: Dr. Weber, tell us about the robots of the future. They'll probably think
_____
                                         1
like us, right?

Dr. Weber: _____. I think _____
                    2   3
the difference between a robot and a person.

Interviewer: _____?
                              4

Dr. Weber: Well, even a smart robot _____ happy or sad.
                                                5

Maybe _____ us smile and learn to smile back
              6

at us, but _____ our feelings. A robot brain
                  7

_____ only one thing at a time, step by step.
          8

And _____ for themselves in new situations.
          9

Interviewer: So _____?
                              10

Dr. Weber: _____ new languages.
                    11

_____ and dance in movies and shows.
          12

But _____ between right and wrong actions.
          13

Humans _____ their instructions.
              14

12 More Uses of *Will*: Robots Don't Do This!

What would you say in these very human situations? Write sentences with *will/won't.*

1. You're at a party, but it's getting late. You decide to leave. Tell your friends.

   I think I'll go home now.

2. You need to mail a letter, but you're busy. Your sister is going to the post office. Make a request.

   Will you mail this letter for me, please?

3. A friend tells you an important secret. Promise never to tell your other friends.

   I promise I'll never tell your secret

4. You have a surprise for a friend. She wants to know what it is. Refuse to tell her.

   I won't tell you

5. A salesperson wants you and your wife to buy a new car. You both decide to think about it this evening. Tell the salesperson.

   We will think about it this evening.

6. Your classmate needs to get to the airport, but she doesn't have a car. Your friend has a car, so he can take her. Make an offer.

   My friend will take you at the airport.

7. You're going to get married! Make a promise to your future husband or wife.

   Will you married my?

8. Make a request to your friends: Invite them to your wedding.

   Will you came to my wedding?

9. Mrs. Cooper found some money in the street. She's a very honest person. Will she decide to keep the money or not? What does she say?

   I will give back the mony

10. A classmate is sick at home. He needs visitors. Make an offer from yourself and a friend.

    I will visit you?

13 Wh- Questions and Answers with Will: Meeting on the Internet

A. Read this Internet advertisement and answer the questions below.

Are You Lonely?

Do You Want to Make New Friends?

Mrs. Matchmaker's Friendship Service

Just log on to Mrs. Matchmaker's Friendship Service. I promise you'll find some friends. Maybe you'll meet your future wife or husband. We'll ask you some questions about your interests. Then we'll match you with the right person. Our experts will help you write your first e-mail message. Your new friends will answer very soon. Do you want more information? Write to us at M1A2TSC4H5.com. Do it today! You won't be sorry.

1. Who(m) will you find through Mrs. Matchmaker's Service?
   A friend.

2. What will they ask you?
   They'll ask you some questions about your interests.

3. What will they do then?
   _____

4. Who will help you with your first e-mail message?
   _____

5. What will happen then?
   _____

6. When will your new friends answer?
   _____

7. How will you get more information?
   _____

8. Where will you write to Mrs. Matchmaker's Service?
   _____

What will I

B. You want more information. Write questions for an e-mail message to
Mrs. Matchmaker. Use *wh-* questions with *will* and the words in parentheses.

1. How much will the service cost? _____
   (The service will cost . . .)
2. Who(m) will I send the payment to? _____
   (I'll send the payment to . . .)
3. What will I say in my e-mail letter? _____
   (I'll say . . . in my e-mail letter.)
4. What will happen next? _____
   (. . . will happen next.)
5. When will I get an answer to my message? _____
   (I'll get an answer to my message . . .)
6. How many friends will you find for me? _____
   (You'll find . . . friends for me.)
7. Who will these friends be? _____
   (These friends will be . . .)
8. Where will they come from? _____
   (They'll come from . . .)

C. Work with a partner. Think of two more *wh-* questions for Mrs. Matchmaker.
Write them below.

9. _____
10. _____

D. Join another pair of partners. Ask and answer each other's questions in Part C.

GRAMMAR BRIEFING 5

Be Going To Versus *Will*

FUNCTION

A. *Be Going To* and *Will*

Use both *be going to* and *will* for predictions about the future.	My life **is going to be** different next year. My life **will be** different next year.

B. *Be Going To*

1. Use *be going to* for immediate expectations about the very near future, based on something happening now.	Look out! You**'re going to fall** into that hole.
2. Use *be going to* for plans made **before** the moment of speaking.	A: What**'s going to happen** now? B: We**'re going to hear** a lecture.

(continued on next page)

C. Will

1. Use *will* for quick decisions (plans made **at** the moment of speaking).	Are you going? Okay, **I'll go** too.
2. Use *will* to talk about willingness or non-willingness for promises, offers, requests, and refusals.	**I'll** always **love** you. Wait. **I'll help** you. **Will** you **buy** me a computer? I **will not buy** you a computer!

GRAMMAR PRACTICE 5

Be Going To Versus Will

 14 ***Be Going To* Versus *Will*: Technical Problems**

Complete the conversations. Use *be going to* or *will/won't* and the words in parentheses.

1. A: Hey, Freddie! <u>Will you stop</u> that noisy video game? I'm on the phone!
        a (you / stop)

    B: Sorry, I didn't know. <u>I will stop</u> it now, okay?
        b (I / stop)

2. A: Where are you putting that message machine?

    B: In a box. <u>I'm going to take</u> it back to the store. It lost all my
        (I / take)

    messages yesterday!

3. A: Our mechanics are busy right now. What do you want to do with your car?

    B: I think <u>I will leave</u> it with you. But I need it back this afternoon!
        a (I / leave)

    A: No problem. I promise <u>we will finish</u> the job today.
        b (we / finish)

4. A: Look at that car! Do you see the smoke?

    B: Oh, no! <u>it going to explode</u>.
        (it / explode)

5. A: Help! My computer isn't working.

    B: Don't worry. <u>I will look</u> at it for you.
        (I / look)

6. A: I bought this camera for $350 last week. Now it doesn't work. I want my money back!

    B: Sorry, sir. We don't give refunds. But <u>you will take</u> another
        a (you / take)

    camera in exchange?

    A: No. <u>I won't take</u> another camera! I want my money back.
        b (I / not take)

7. A: I missed the movie on Channel 6 last night. I really wanted to see it!

    B: Well, _they are going to show_ it again at eight o'clock tonight.
        a (they / show)

    A: Really? _Are you going to watch_ it?
        b (you / watch)

    B: Yes. Do you want to come to my house?

    A: Sure. _I will see_ you tonight, then.
        c (I / see)

Present Progressive and Simple Present for Future Time

FUNCTION

A. Present Progressive

1. The present progressive is sometimes used to describe specific **plans** for the future. A time expression usually shows that the activity is in the future.

    A: What **are** you **doing tonight**?
    B: **I'm meeting** my uncle for dinner.

2. Use *be going to* (not the present progressive) for **predictions** about the future.

    It **is** probably **going to rain** tomorrow.
    NOT: It ~~is probably raining~~ tomorrow.

B. Simple Present

1. The simple present is sometimes used to describe future **schedules** that are fixed and regular—for example, in class programs and in timetables for buses, trains, and airplanes. A time expression usually shows that the schedule is in the future.

    My new class **starts next Monday**.

2. Pairs of verbs commonly used with the simple present to express future time include:

    Flight 202 **departs** at 9:00.
    The game **starts** in about three minutes.

    • *Arrive, leave/depart.*

    • *Begin, finish.*

    • *Start, end.*

    • *Open, close.*

Remember! Use *be going to* or the present progressive for **plans** about the future.

> I **am going to visit** Raul tomorrow. OR I **am visiting** Raul tomorrow.

Use only *be going to* for **predictions**.

> It **is going to rain** tomorrow.
> NOT: It ~~is raining~~ tomorrow.

GRAMMAR PRACTICE 6

Present Progressive and Simple Present for Future Time

15 **Future Versus Present Meaning:** My Computer Date

Raul's computer is changing his life! Read Raul's conversation with his friend Jan. Above the **boldfaced** verbs, write **P** if they are talking about present time or **F** if they are talking about future time.

1. Raul: Why **are** you **running**, Jan? [P]

2. Jan: I'**m going to be** [F] late for class! It **starts** in a few minutes. But first I **want** [P] to buy some tickets for the concert. I'**m going** [P] to the ticket office right now.

3. Raul: Oh, you'**re going** [F] to that laser music concert tonight. **Is it** [F] at 7:30?

4. Jan: Yes. **Are** you **coming** [F] tonight too? I'**ll get** [F] you a ticket.

5. Raul: No, thanks. I'**m staying** [F] home this evening. I'**m chatting** [F] to my new girlfriend online tonight.

6. Jan: An online date? You'**re joking**! [P]

7. Raul: No, really. We met through an Internet friendship service. My girlfriend's name is Linda. She **lives** [P] in Spain. I'**ll tell** [F] you all about her.

8. Jan: Sure! But not now. The ticket office **closes** [F] in five minutes. And it **doesn't open** again before the concert.

9. Raul: Look! There's your class instructor. He'**s coming** [P] this way.

10. Jan: Uh-oh. I'**m going to go** [F]. I'**ll call** [F] you tonight, okay? After the concert.

16 Present Progressive for Future Time: Making a Date

Jan wants to chat online with Linh, a Taiwanese student in another American city. Work with a partner. Student A looks at Jan's schedule. Student B looks at Linh's schedule. Find a time when they can talk online. Use the present progressive tense. Use time expressions (*on Saturday, at noon, in the morning,* etc.) as appropriate.

Example: A: What is Jan doing next Friday evening?
B: He's seeing a movie with Bill. Is Linh free on Saturday?
A: She's visiting her grandmother in the morning.

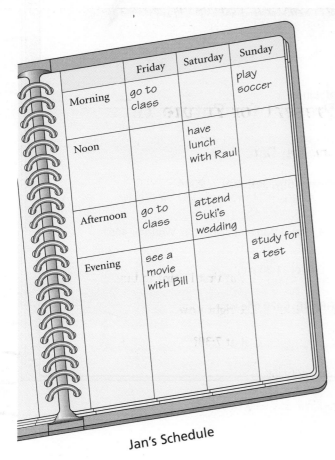

	Friday	Saturday	Sunday
Morning	go to class		play soccer
Noon		have lunch with Raul	
Afternoon	go to class	attend Suki's wedding	
Evening	see a movie with Bill		study for a test

Jan's Schedule

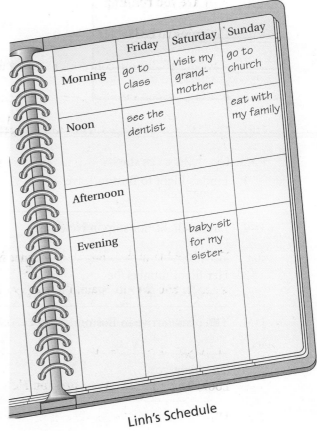

	Friday	Saturday	Sunday
Morning	go to class	visit my grand-mother	go to church
Noon	see the dentist		eat with my family
Afternoon			
Evening		baby-sit for my sister	

Linh's Schedule

17 **Simple Present for Future Time:** An Important Trip

A. Raul's new girlfriend, Linda, is coming to meet him in Boston. Write statements about Linda's flight schedule. Use the words given and the simple present tense.

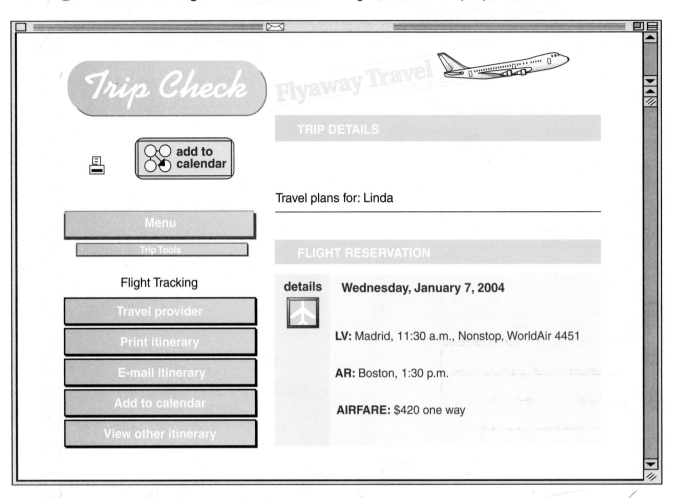

1. Linda's flight to Boston/leave

   Linda's flight to Boston leaves on January 7.

2. Linda's flight/not stop in New York

   Linda's flight is not going to stop in New York.

3. Her flight number/be

   Her flight number is going to be 4451.

4. The plane/arrive in Boston

   The plane is going to arrive in Boston

5. The flight/cost

   The flight is going to cost $420 one away.

   the plane we arrive in Boston

   the flight cost $420 one away

B. Linda is planning her return trip to Madrid. Work with a partner. Discuss dates, times, and airfares (prices) for the two flights in the advertisement. Which is the better flight for Linda? Write about the schedule you choose. Write sentences like the ones in Part A.

Trip Check   Flyaway Travel

TRIP DETAILS

add to calendar

Travel plans for: Linda

Menu

Trip Tools

Flight Tracking

Travel provider

Print itinerary

E-mail itinerary

Add to calendar

View other itinerary

FLIGHT RESERVATION

details

Tuesday, January 20, 2004

LV: Boston, 7:35 p.m., Nonstop, WorldAir 3490

AR: Madrid, 7:00 a.m., Wednesday

AIRFARE: $420 one way

details

Tuesday, January 13, 2004

LV: Boston, 9:00 p.m., Nonstop, WorldAir 1120

AR: New York, 9:45 p.m.

LV: New York, 1:05 a.m., Wednesday
Nonstop, SunAir 204

AR: Madrid, 12:30 p.m.

AIRFARE: $400 one way

---

1. _____
2. _____
3. _____
4. _____
5. _____

C. Can you find a better flight for Linda? Work with a partner. On the Internet, research some airline fares and schedules between Madrid and Boston. Then share your findings with the rest of the class. Who found the best fares and schedules?

18 Present Progressive or Simple Present for Future Time: A Happy Ending

Raul found his future wife on the Internet! Raul and Linda decide to have a virtual wedding and invite their friends to "attend" the wedding online. Complete their electronic wedding invitation. Use the present progressive or the simple present.

From: Raul and Linda
Sent: 3/13/04
To: Everyone
Subject: Come to Our Wedding! Fly with Us to the Moon!

Raul and Linda _are goin to get_ married on May 20! We _are going to rent_ a virtual
            1 (get)   2 (rent)

spaceship, and _they will go_ to the moon for our special day. We _are going to take_
            3 (go)   4 (take)   *taking*

our friends and families with us. Here's the schedule. Our virtual spaceship _we are going to leave_
                                                                          5 (leave) *leaves*

at 10:00 in the morning and _will land_ at 10:15. The wedding ____is____
                          6 (land) *lands*   7 (be)

at the Crater Chapel, at 11:30. The reception _begins_ at 2:00 p.m. Our families
                                          8 (begin)

are give us a great reception party! They _will provide_ food, drinks, and
9 (give)   10 (provide)

a mariachi band. ____are____ you ____come____ with us? We hope so!
                                       11 (come)

Raul and Linda

19 Talking About the Future: Discussion

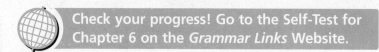 In small groups, discuss these questions.

1. Will Raul and Linda have a good future? What will happen after the wedding?

2. What do you think about virtual friendships, dates, and weddings?

3. Are people going to live more and more in a "virtual" world?

4. Is it a good idea to meet new people on the Internet? Is this activity ever dangerous?

Check your progress! Go to the Self-Test for Chapter 6 on the *Grammar Links* Website.

Chapter 7

Future Time Clauses; Conditionals

Introductory Task: Technology—Friend or Enemy?

 A. Two politicians, Senator O'Leary and Senator Fallows, are discussing technology and the problems of the world. Listen to their discussion. Write the words you hear. Use the correct forms of the verbs in the box.

be	clean	fish	have	✓need
cause	destroy	✓go	learn	use
control	(not) find	have	live	

O'Leary: Technology is destroying our environment—the world we live in. Cars and factories

send clouds of smoke into the air. Soon, people _are going to need_
₁

smog masks when they _go_ _____ outside. Factories are
₂

putting dangerous waste into the water. When we _____
₃

in the rivers, we _____ anything safe to eat.
₄

Technology is also using up the world's natural energy. We are burning forests,

Coal

coal, and oil in huge power plants. How _____ we

_____ in the world after we _____
₅   ₆

these forms of energy? Technology _____ more and
₇

more problems until we _____ it.
₈

Fallows: I disagree. If we _____ technology, we
₉

_____ progress. Technology means new discoveries, for
₁₀

example, in medicine and space research. Technology will help solve the problems of the

environment. For example, the Center for Clean Technology—the CCT—in Los Angeles is

developing new technology to attack pollution. If the CCT _____
₁₁

successful, this technology _____ the waste
12

in our air and water. The CCT is also studying uranium as a form of

energy. If we _____ to control uranium, we
13

_____ it for energy and save our forests, and coal and
14

oil supplies. Yes, Senator O'Leary. Technology will bring good changes for the future.

> *smog masks* = face covers to protect you from bad things in the air. *waste* = useless
> material. *uranium* = a radioactive element that produces nuclear energy.

B. Work in small groups. Discuss the conversation in Part A. Which statements do you agree with? Which statements do you disagree with? Do you agree more with Senator O'Leary or with Senator Fallows?

Future Time Clauses

FORM

A. Overview

Some sentences about future time have two clauses: a main clause and a future time clause. The future time clause begins with a time expression. The main clause does not.

time clause	main clause
When the bus stops,	I will get off.

B. Statements

TIME CLAUSE			MAIN CLAUSE			
TIME EXPRESSION	SUBJECT	SIMPLE PRESENT	SUBJECT	*WILL/ BE GOING TO*	BASE VERB	
When	I	**know**,	I	will	**tell**	you.
				am going to		
After	he	**leaves**,	she	won't	**stay**.	
				isn't going to		

1. The time clause, the main clause, or both clauses can be negative.

   > When I**'m not** busy, I'll call you.
   > When I finish this project, I **won't be** busy.
   > When I**'m not** busy, I **won't be** tired.

2. A time clause can come before or after the main clause. Use a comma (**,**) after the time clause when the time clause comes first.

   > **When I know,** I'm going to tell you.
   > I'm going to tell you **when I know.**

(continued on next page)

C. Questions

Questions are formed in the main clause. The time clause does not change.

Are you going to tell me when you know?

When you know, **what will you tell me**?

FUNCTION

A. Overview

Future time clauses tell the order (first or second) of two actions or situations in the future.

first action   second action
When the bus stops, <u>I will get off</u>.

B. Time Expressions

1. *When, after,* and *as soon as* introduce the action that will happen first.

   As soon as means that the second action will happen **immediately** after the first action.

   When I know, I'm going to tell you. (First I'm going to know; then I'm going to tell you.)

   As soon as I know, I will tell you. (I will tell you right away.)

2. *Before* introduces the action or a situation that will happen second.

   Before I come, I'm going to call you. (First I'm going to call you; then I'm going to come.)

3. *Until* introduces an action or situation that stops another action. The main clause action starts first and continues to the time of the time clause action.

   I'll stay **until** you tell me to leave. (I'll stay; then you'll tell me to leave, and I won't stay anymore.)

GRAMMAR HOT SPOT!

Remember! Use the simple present in the future time clause.

When I know, I'll tell you.
   NOT: When I ~~will know~~, I'll tell you.

Future Time Clauses

1 **Future Time Clauses:** Verb Forms

A. Complete the sentences with the correct form of the verbs in parentheses.
Use *will* when necessary.

1. He _will come_ home as soon as he _finishes_
   (come)   (finish)
   his work.

2. As soon as we ____see____ him, we __will__ __give__
   (see)   (give)
   him your message.

3. I __will not stay__ with you until I _____ better.
   (not / stay)   (feel)

4. Before you _____, I _____ that
   (go)   (get)
   book for you.

5. They _____ you after they _____
   (call)   (arrive)
   in London.

B. Complete the sentences with the correct form of the verbs in parentheses.
Use *be going to* when necessary.

1. She _'s going to be_ rich before she __'s__
   (be)   (be)
   30 years old.

2. After the spacecraft ____landed____ it _____
   (land)   (send)
   a message back to Earth.

3. Until you _____ "please," I _____
   (say)   (not / give)
   it to you.

4. When we _____ this project, we _____
   (finish)   (have)
   a big party!

5. She _____ very happy when she _____
   (not / be)   (hear)
   the news.

2 Future Time Clauses: Function

Read the underlined sentences. Write *1* above the action that happens first in each one. Then check (✓) the sentence that gives the same information.

1. <u>He's going to eat. Before that, he's going to take a shower.</u>
   [1 above "he's going to take a shower"]

   a. He's going to eat before he takes a shower. ☐

   b. He's going to take a shower before he eats. ☑

2. <u>They're going to get tired. Until that time, they're going to play.</u>
   [1 above "get tired"]

   a. They're going to get tired until they play. ☑

   b. They're going to play until they get tired. ☐

3. <u>I will tell you the secret. Will you be angry with me after that?</u>
   [1 above "angry"]

   a. Will you be angry with me after I tell you the secret? ☑

   b. After you are angry with me, will I tell you the secret? ☐

4. <u>I'll clean the kitchen. Then we'll have dinner right away.</u>
   [1 above "kitchen"]

   a. As soon as I clean the kitchen, we'll have dinner. ☑

   b. I'll clean the kitchen as soon as we have dinner. ☐

5. <u>She will know him better. Until that time, she won't go out with him.</u>
   [1 above "go"]

   a. She won't go out with him until she knows him better. ☑

   b. She won't know him better until she goes out with him. ☐

3 Future Time Clauses and Time Expressions: Presidential Promises

A. Senator O'Leary and Senator Fallows want to be president of their country. They are making promises to the voters. Combine the pairs of sentences below. Write the clauses in the order given. Add commas where necessary.

B. Work in small groups. Look at the promises of each senator in Part A. Discuss their promises. Who do you think will become president? Why?

Senator O'Leary:

1. I'm going to be president. I'm going to protect the environment.
   After *I'm president, I'm going to protect the environment.*

2. I won't rest. Our country will use less energy.
   _____
   until _____

3. I'll form my government. We'll pass clean air laws.
   As soon as _____

4. We'll fight big industries. Their factories will destroy nature.
   _____
   _____ when

5. We'll organize free city buses. People won't need so many cars.
   After _____

6. We're going to control technology. Technology is going to control us.
   _____
   _____ before

Senator Fallows:

7. You won't be sorry. You will vote for me.
   You won't be sorry _____
   when *you vote for me.*

8. I'm going to work. Our country is going to be a world leader.
   _____
   until _____

9. Other countries will look at us. They'll see great technological progress.
   When _____

10. This progress is going to happen. We're going to develop our medical,
    space, and energy-production industries.
    _____
    after _____

11. I'm going to support these industries. You're going to make me your
    president. _____
    as soon as _____

12. I will finish my presidency. I will lead you well into the twenty-first century.
    Before _____

4 Future Time Clauses and Time Expressions: Travel to Mars

 Senator Fallows is reading about NASA's plans for future travel to Mars. (NASA is the U.S. National Aeronautics and Space Agency.) Work as a class. Write as many sentences as you can about NASA's schedule. Use future time clauses with *after*, *as soon as*, *before*, *until*, and *when*.

Examples: After Spacecraft 1 goes to Mars, it's going to stay there.

The rocks will stay on Mars until Spacecraft 2 brings them back to Earth.

Schedule for Travel to Mars

December 2005	Spacecraft 1: Go to Mars. Send out robot.
	Robot: Prepare rocks for return flight.
	Robot: Stay on Mars.
2006 or 2007	Spacecraft 2: Pick up rocks from 2005 flight. Bring them back to Earth.
After 2007	More spacecrafts: Make many return trips to Mars.
	NASA: Prepare for human travel.
After 2012	NASA: Send humans to Mars.

See the *Grammar Links* Website for more information about NASA.

5 Future Time Clauses—Questions and Answers: Debate

 A. Senators O'Leary and Fallows are having a debate (a public discussion) on TV. Senator O'Leary sees many problems with Senator Fallows' ideas about technology. Write Senator O'Leary's questions to Senator Fallows. Combine the sentences below. Replace the **boldfaced** time expressions with *after*, *as soon as*, *before*, *until*, and *when*.

1. Spacecrafts will have accidents in space. What will NASA do **then**?

   When spacecrafts have accidents in space, what will NASA do?

   OR

   What will NASA do when spacecrafts have accidents in space?

2. These accidents will happen. Will NASA send help **right away**?

   Will NASA send help as soon as these accidents happen?

3. We will send people to Mars. Will we solve the problems on Earth **before then**?

   Will we solve the problems on Earth as soon as we
   Wil
   will send people to Mars.

4. We will start to use uranium for energy. Will we learn to control nuclear power **before then**?

Will we learn to control nuclear as soon as we will start to use uranium for energy.

5. We will use uranium. Where will we dump the radioactive waste **after that**?

where will we dump the radioactive wast, we will use uranium.

6. All our fish will die. Will submarines dump oil in the oceans **up to that time**?

Will submarines dump oil in the oceans, All our fish will die

7. Our children are going to grow up. How will we find the answers to pollution **before then**?

8. Our children will start school. Will they become technology addicts **right away**?

Will they become technology addicts as soo as our children will start school

9. Machines are going to take all our jobs. Will scientists keep building robots **up to that time**?

Will scientists keep building robots, the Machines are going to take all our jobs.

10. Robots are going to make serious mistakes. What will happen **then**?

When Robots are going to make serious mistakes, what will happen. serious mistakes.

B. How did Senator Fallows answer Senator O'Leary's questions in Part A? Work in small groups. Ask one another the questions, and think of good answers. If you can't think of an answer, say, "I don't know."

Examples: A: When spacecrafts have accidents in space, what will NASA do?

B: They'll bring the spacecrafts back to Earth.

C: Will NASA send help as soon as these accidents happen?

D: Yes, it will. NASA will have a special ambulance service.

6 Future Time Clauses with *Be Going to* and *Will*: Role-Play

A. Divide into two groups. One group plays the role of Senator O'Leary. You want to fight pollution and control technology. The other group plays the role of Senator Fallows. You want to build technology and use it to solve the world's problems. Write questions to ask the other group. Use future time clauses, *be going to* or *will*, and time expressions. Use the ideas in the Introductory Task and the exercises to help you.

Examples:
(Question for Senator O'Leary): Will you take away our cars as soon as you are president?

(Question for Senator Fallows): What's going to happen to our jobs when you develop all this technology?

B. Role-play the debate between the two senators. Each group asks and answers their questions from Part A.

C. Write about the class debate. In your opinion, which senator has the best promises and answers? Why? Write a paragraph of at least five sentences.

See the *Grammar Links* Website for a complete model paragraph for this assignment.

Factual and Future Conditionals

FORM

A. Factual Conditionals

A factual conditional sentence has a main clause and an *if* clause. Use the **simple present** tense in both clauses.

IF CLAUSE				**MAIN CLAUSE**		
IF	SUBJECT	SIMPLE PRESENT		SUBJECT	SIMPLE PRESENT	
If	you	**heat**	water,	it	**boils**.	

B. Future Conditionals

A future conditional sentence also has a main clause and an *if* clause. Use the **simple present** tense in the *if* clause. Use the **future** with *will* or *be going to* in the main clause.

IF CLAUSE			**MAIN CLAUSE**			
IF	SUBJECT	SIMPLE PRESENT	SUBJECT	*WILL /BE GOING TO*	BASE VERB	
If	you	**leave,**	John	**will/is going to**	be	sad.

C. Negative Conditionals

The *if* clause, the main clause, or both clauses can be negative.

If I **don't** work on the weekend, I go out.

If I **don't** work this weekend, I **won't** stay at home.

If I work this weekend, I **won't** go out.

D. Order of Clauses

The *if* clause can come before or after the main clause. Use a comma after an *if* clause at the beginning of a sentence.

If you leave, Jody will cry.

Jody will cry **if you leave**.

(continued on next page)

A. Factual Conditionals

1. A factual conditional tells **what usually or always happens** under certain conditions (situations). The *if* clause describes the condition. The main clause tells the usual result.

   > condition   usual result
   > If I have time, I walk to work.

   > condition   usual result
   > If I heat water, it boils.

2. *When* can be used instead of *if* in factual conditionals. The meaning is the same.

   > Water boils **if** you heat it. = Water boils **when** you heat it.

B. Future Conditionals

A future conditional predicts **what will happen in the future** under certain conditions. The *if* clause gives the condition. The main clause predicts the result.

> condition   predicted result
> If it's hot tomorrow, we'll go to the beach.

> condition   predicted result
> If it's hot tomorrow, we're going to go to the beach.

GRAMMAR HOTSPOT!

Remember! Use the simple present in the *if* clause of future conditionals, even though the meaning is future.

> We'll go to the beach if it **is** hot tomorrow.
> **NOT**: We'll go the beach if it ~~will be~~ hot tomorrow.

Factual and Future Conditionals

7 **Recognizing Verb Tenses in Factual and Future Conditionals: Animal Protection I**

Listen to Senator O'Leary's speech about animal protection. Write the words you hear.

Technology is harming our environment. Without a clean environment, many animals

won't survive. If we __continue__ to pollute the air with our cars and airplanes,

1

we _____ many kinds of birds forever. If they _____ clean air,

2   3

birds suffer and sometimes die. The "noise pollution" we make is also bad for birds.

If there _____ too much noise around them,

4

birds _____ away and never come back.

5

Pollution also hurts other animals. The Arctic polar bear is one of

these animals. When we pollute the air, it _____ warmer.

6

When warm air _____ ice, the ice melts. If ice continues

7

to melt in the Arctic, polar bears _____ their home.

8

If this _____, they will not survive.

9

If you elect me president, I _____ hard for the future of all animals.

10

My government will pass a clean air law. This is a promise I make to you. And if Senator

O'Leary _____ a promise, he _____ it!

11   12

Polar Bear and Ice

> *survive* = continue to live. *suffer* = feel pain or discomfort.

8 **Conditions and Results in Factual and Future Conditionals: Animal Protection II**

Look again at Senator O'Leary's speech in Exercise 7.

A. Some of his sentences are factual conditionals. They talk about what usually or always happens if a condition exists. Write the conditions and results in the columns:

Condition	Result
they don't have clean air	*birds suffer and sometimes die*
_____	_____
_____	_____
_____	_____
_____	_____

B. Some of Senator O'Leary's sentences are future conditionals. They predict what will happen under certain conditions. Write the conditions and his predicted results in the columns:

Condition	**Result**
we continue to pollute the air	*we will lose many kinds of birds*
_____	_____
_____	_____

9 **Identifying Factual and Future Conditionals:** The Manatee, an Animal in Danger

Read the article. Underline the seven conditional sentences. Label them *Factual* (about usual results) or *Future* (about predicted results).

If you go to a marine zoo in Florida, you will probably see a manatee (a "sea cow"). You will almost certainly see manatees if you look for them at Disney World or Sea World.

Manatees weigh up to 3,000 pounds and grow up to 13 feet long if they reach full size. They are mammals, and they eat only plants.

When they need to protect themselves from boats, manatees dive under water and hold their breath. They can hold their breath for 20 minutes! However, manatees swim slowly. If a boat is moving fast, they don't have time to go under water. Almost all wild manatees have scars from boats.

Manatees are an endangered species. If people don't protect them, they will become extinct. The Save the Manatee Club sends information if you ask for it.

---

marine zoo = zoo for sea animals. *mammals* = warm-blooded animals that usually have hair or fur. *scar* = mark left on the skin after an injury. *endangered species* = animals in danger of no longer existing.

 Are you interested in protecting endangered species? See the *Grammar Links* Website for more information.

10 Writing Factual Conditional Sentences: Animal Protection III

A. Animals don't wait for humans to protect them. They also protect themselves. Combine the sentences in brackets [ ] to form factual conditionals with *if* or *when*. Use the **boldfaced** sentence for the *if/when* clause. Do not change the order of the clauses. Use commas where necessary.

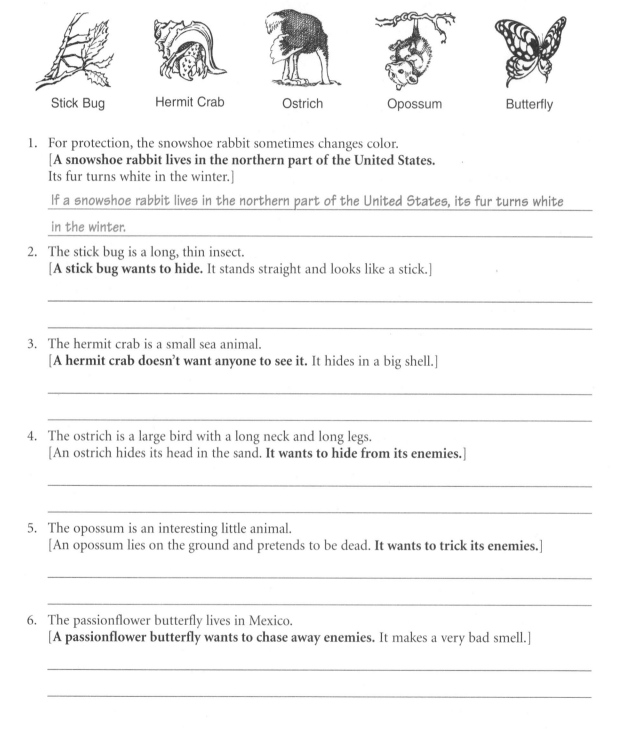

Stick Bug   Hermit Crab   Ostrich   Opossum   Butterfly

1. For protection, the snowshoe rabbit sometimes changes color.
   [**A snowshoe rabbit lives in the northern part of the United States.**
   Its fur turns white in the winter.]

   If a snowshoe rabbit lives in the northern part of the United States, its fur turns white
   in the winter.

2. The stick bug is a long, thin insect.
   [**A stick bug wants to hide.** It stands straight and looks like a stick.]

   _____

   _____

3. The hermit crab is a small sea animal.
   [**A hermit crab doesn't want anyone to see it.** It hides in a big shell.]

   _____

   _____

4. The ostrich is a large bird with a long neck and long legs.
   [An ostrich hides its head in the sand. **It wants to hide from its enemies.**]

   _____

   _____

5. The opossum is an interesting little animal.
   [An opossum lies on the ground and pretends to be dead. **It wants to trick its enemies.**]

   _____

   _____

6. The passionflower butterfly lives in Mexico.
   [**A passionflower butterfly wants to chase away enemies.** It makes a very bad smell.]

   _____

   _____

B. Discuss as a class: Do humans use any protection behaviors similar to those in Part A? Which ones? Use factual conditional sentences.

11 Writing Future Conditional Sentences: Animal Superstitions

We know that human technology affects animals. But some people also believe animals affect us and our behavior, sometimes in very strange ways. Here are some superstitions about the effects of animals on humans.

A. Make future conditional sentences with the words given. Use *if* in the **boldfaced** part of the sentence. Use commas where necessary.

1. **a black cat walk in front of you**/you/have bad luck.

   If a black cat walks in front of you, you will have bad luck.

2. you grow warts (bumps) on your fingers/**you/touch a toad**.

   _____

3. **you keep a rabbit's foot in your pocket**/you/be lucky.

   _____

4. **a bat bite you**/you/become a bat.

   _____

Bat

5. you/have good luck/**a cricket visit your house**.

   _____

Cricket

superstition = belief based on magic or chance.

B. Discuss as a class: Have you ever heard any of the superstitions in Part A? Do you believe them? Why or why not?

Worm

C. Make up your own superstitions about how animals affect us. Write future conditional sentences.

Spider

1. If you _____ a worm, _____.
2. _____ if you _____ a spider.
3. If a fish _____, you _____.
4. You _____ if a horse _____.

Add two superstitions of your own. Use superstitions you have heard, or make them up.

5. _____ if you _____

   a _____.

6. _____ if you _____

   a _____.

D. Work in small groups. Discuss the sentences you wrote in Part C. Were any of your sentences similar or the same? Which ones?

12 Negative Conditionals: RoboCat—Pet of the Future

Randy is at a pet shop. Complete his conversation with the salesperson.

Randy: I'm looking for a pet for my mother. If she has a pet, maybe she

___won't be_____ so lonely.
      1 (not / be)

Salesperson: What a wonderful idea. I have the perfect pet for your mother. If you buy this pet,

you _____ sorry.
        2 (not / be)

Randy: That? What is it?

Salesperson: It's RoboCat. Go ahead. Pick it up.

Randy: But . . . it's a machine. And it looks dangerous. If I touch it, it

_____ soft and cuddly. It looks cold and sharp.
   3 (not / be going to be)

Salesperson: Shhh! This RoboCat is very sensitive. If you _____
                                                              4 (not / be)

careful, you will make it feel bad. And it won't hurt you if you

_____ it. This RoboCat is a very
   5 (not / hurt)

gentle, very friendly pet.

Randy: Friendly?

Salesperson: Yes. If you're nice to it, it _____ you.
                                            6 (never / leave)

And if you forget to feed it, it _____ hungry.
                                    7 (not get)

It can live forever without food.

Randy: Okay. But if my mother doesn't like this pet, she _____
                                                          8 (not / want)

to keep it.

Salesperson: If your mother _____ RoboCat, we'll give you back
                              9 (not /like)

your money. But your mother will love it. If she _____
                                                   10 (not / love)

this fine little pet, I'll be very surprised.

13 **Editing:** Mom's Best Friend

Correct the errors in Randy's note. There are seven errors with factual and future conditionals. The first one is corrected for you.

Dear Mom,

Say hello to your new pet—RoboCat! When I left, she was under the refrigerator. If you ~~will~~ see her, you will love her. She is a wonderful pet. If you don't like her, we are take her back to the pet store. But I think you will like her. And she loves people. When people will be nice to RoboCat, she is nice to people, too. She is also easy to take care of. If you will forget to feed her, she will still be happy. And just like other cats, she makes a noise when she will be happy. When she sounds like a car engine she is happy. Oh—and I think she is going to have babies. If she has babies. You will have about 100 more little RoboCats to keep you company soon!

Love,

Randy

14 **Factual and Future Conditionals:** Sell That Pet!

 You work in a pet shop. Choose one of these pets. Write an advertisement of at least five sentences for it. Use at least two factual and two future conditionals. Use the picture and the facts about your pet to help you.

 Tarantula

 Flea

 Snake

Tarantula	Flea	Snake
bites only when you frighten it	likes to do jumping tricks	has a beautiful silver coat
will eat flies and other pests	will be happy living in your rug	will eat mice and other pests
is soft and furry	enjoys the company of cats and dogs	loves to wrap around you and hug you
won't make noise	won't make noise	makes an interesting hissing noise
has eight beautiful deep black eyes	won't take up much space	has two beautiful narrow green eyes

Example:

You'll love this tarantula. If you don't like noise, it's the pet for you. It is very quiet.

If you don't frighten it, it won't bite you.

 See the *Grammar Links* Website for a complete model paragraph for this assignment.

Check your progress! Go to the Self-Test for Chapter 7 on the *Grammar Links* Website.

Wrap-up Activities

1 Technology News: EDITING

Correct the errors in this advertisement. There are 12 errors with the future tense and with conditionals. The first one is corrected for you. After you finish, guess what the advertisement is talking about. (The answer to the puzzle is on page 132).

INTRODUCING A WONDERFUL INVENTION!

What are you doing next Friday evening?

Are you free?

Come to our demonstration!

*N*ext Friday evening, we are presenting a wonderful piece of information technology. You're going to love it! In fact, you're probably going to buy it as soon as you will see it. This technology will help you with college examinations. It is introducing you to wonderful new worlds. Perhaps it will to teach you a new language. When you'll need to find some information, you'll open a cover at the back, and you'll be see an "index." The index will direct you to the correct information.

You'll save energy if you will use this technology. You won't need batteries or electric wires—just your eyes. If you move your eyes over the information, it will coming straight to you.

It's easy to use—no instructions or programs. It's strong, too—it doesn't break when you will drop it or sit on it. Best of all, it's cheap! After you see the low price, you'll be going to buy two or three.

Our demonstration is at the public library. It starts at 6:00 p.m. and will finishes at 7:30. We'll going to show you this technology and answer your questions. Before you are leaving, you will test several examples. Please come!

What is this advertisement talking about? _____

_____

2 Ideas About the Future: SPEAKING

Step 1 Interview a student in another class. Ask what he or she expects to find in the world 20 years from now. Ask about jobs, nature, homes, and so on. Ask how technology will change the world.

Step 2 Report back to the class and compare the interviews. What did the students from the other classes say about technology?

3 Utopia: SPEAKING

Step 1 Work in small groups. Imagine you have the power to make laws or change anything you want in the world! Make a list of five plans and promises for your "utopia"—your perfect world.

Step 2 Share your ideas with the class. Are there some ideas that you all agree about?

Examples:

When children finish school, we'll send them to live in another country for one year.

We're going to teach everybody in the world to read and write.

We won't spend any more money on space travel.

4 Designing a Pet: SPEAKING/WRITING

Step 1 Draw a picture of your ideal future pet. What will it look like? Will it be alive, or will it be a robot? Or, like Roboroach, will it be half and half?

Step 2 On a different piece of paper, write a paragraph about your new pet. Write at least five sentences. Describe your pet carefully. Use the future tense, and use conditionals in your paragraph.

Example:

My ideal pet of the future will be half dog and half cat. If I need company, it won't

run away and hide. . . .

 See *the Grammar Links* Website for a complete model paragraph for this activity.

Step 3 Mix up all of the pictures and all of the paragraphs.

Step 4 Match the pictures to the paragraphs. Discuss the ideal animals as a class. Which ones seem the most creative? The funniest? The most interesting? Why?

Nouns, Articles, Quantifiers, and Pronouns

TOPIC FOCUS
Travel and Transportation

UNIT OBJECTIVES

▪ **proper and common nouns**
(*Dan Evans* is a *pilot*. He flies *airplanes*.)

▪ **count and noncount nouns**
(*Trains* were very popular in the 1800s. *Transportation* by train was fast and convenient.)

▪ **articles**
(She bought *a* banana and *an* apple. She took *the* apple on *the* train with her.)

▪ **quantifiers**
(*Many* people enjoy walking. They don't need *much* equipment to walk.)

▪ **pronouns and possessive adjectives**
(Martin loves to travel. *He* goes all over the world on *his* bicycle.)

Henry Ford in an Early Model Automobile

Grammar in Action

🎧 Reading and Listening: Travel Through Time

Read and listen. Write the words you hear.

1 _Five hundred_₁ thousand years ago, _____₂
people traveled on foot. _____₃ people still enjoy traveling on foot.
However, _____₄ methods of transportation now exist.

2 About six thousand years ago, people learned to ride animals. Horses were
_____₅ high-speed method of transportation at that time!
Later, humans invented _____₆ wheel, and horses also began
pulling carts and wagons. By _____₇ year 1900, horse-drawn
wagons were very common in _____₈ towns and
_____₉ cities of many countries.

3 In the early 1800s, _____₁₀ began to change. Inventors
developed steam engines for trains. This was _____₁₁ special.
_____₁₂ enjoyed riding on trains!

4 Then, in 1908, Henry Ford invented _____₁₃ Model T
automobile. _____₁₄ entered the "Age of Automobiles," and
_____₁₅ world changed forever. Soon automobiles replaced
trains for long-distance travel. In 1880, there were no automobiles. Eighty years
later, there were 95 million of _____₁₆!

5 In 1903, Orville Wright made _____₁₇ first flight in an airplane.
People began to fly long distances. Now the world seemed very small, and people began to
dream about traveling in space. For _____₁₈ years, space travel was
_____₁₉ people read about in books or saw in science-fiction movies.
Then, in _____₂₀ 1960s, _____₂₁ suddenly happened.
_____₂₂ Russian astronaut circled _____₂₃ earth
in _____₂₄ spaceship in 1961. _____₂₅ years
later, in 1969, astronauts were walking on _____₂₆ moon!
Where will we travel next?

Wheel

Wagon

Steam Engine

Astronaut

Think About Grammar

A. Look at the words you wrote in paragraph 1. Write them in Column A.

Look at the words you wrote in paragraph 2. Write them in Column B.

Look at the words you wrote in paragraph 3. Write them in Column C.

Look at the words you wrote in paragraph 4. Write them in Column D.

Look at the words you wrote in paragraph 5. Write them in the correct column: A, B, C, or D.

Column A	Column B	Column C	Column D
Quantifiers and Numbers	Articles	Indefinite Pronouns	Pronouns and Possessive Adjectives
Five hundred			

B. Look at the reading and at the words you wrote in Part A. Circle **T** if the statement is true and **F** if the statement is false.

1. Words that come before nouns and tell *how much* or *how many* are quantifiers or numbers.　　T　　F

2. There are at least two different articles in English.　　T　　F

3. Pronouns always come just before verbs.　　T　　F

135

a, an : use for singular nouns.

Nouns and Articles

Introductory Task: Always Moving Forward!

A. Read this article from a health and fitness magazine. The author is a 78-year-old woman who walks everywhere.

Always Moving Forward!

By Gertrude Jacobs

Walking is the best way to travel. I work at a **bank** three miles from my house. I walk to work every day, and it's very good exercise. It's also a lot of fun because the **children** in my neighborhood sometimes walk with me. We walk and talk together.

You don't need expensive equipment when you walk. I have good shoes, a coat, and an **umbrella** for bad weather. I don't have a **purse**. I carry a **backpack** instead. It holds all the **things** I need: the **keys** to my house, the **wallet** my son gave me, pictures of the **people** in my family, and five or six dollars, in case of an **emergency**. Sometimes I put an **apple** or an **orange** in my backpack, too. When I get hungry on the way home from work, I just stop and have a **snack**!

I never take a **bus** or drive a **car**! The **buses** in this town cause too much pollution, and the **car** I own causes pollution, too. Besides, the **cars** I see on my way to work are standing still in traffic. I never stand still. I'm always moving forward.

---

equipment = things needed for an activity. *purse* = bag for carrying personal items.
backpack = bag carried on the back. *emergency* = sudden, serious situation.
snack = food eaten between meals.

 See the *Grammar Links* Website for more information about walking and your health.

B. Look at the **boldfaced** words in Part A. They are all nouns.

[handwritten, top right: bus, car / emergency]

1. Which of these nouns are singular (only one person, place, or thing)?
   Write them here.
   bank, *car, apple, orange, umbrella, snack, backpack*

2. Which of these nouns are plural (more than one person, place, or thing)?
   Write them here.
   children, *people, buses, cars, things, keys*

3. Is this statement true (T) or false (F)? Circle the correct answer.

   All plural nouns in English end in -s.   T   (F)

C. Each **boldfaced** noun has the word *a, an,* or *the* in front of it.

1. Write each **boldfaced** noun in the column that matches the word in front of it.

a	an	the
bank	umbrella	children
purse	emergency	keys
backpack	apple	things
snack	orange	wallet
bus	hour	people
car		buses
		car
		cars

2. Are these statements true (T) or false (F)? Circle the correct answer.

   a. The *a* column and the *an* column have plural nouns in them.   T   F

   b. The *the* column has singular nouns and plural nouns in it.   T   (F)

D. *A* and *an* mean the same thing in English. Look at the nouns in Part C. Some nouns have *a* in front of them, and some nouns have *an*. Why do you think this is true?

_____

Proper Nouns and Common Nouns

FORM and FUNCTION

A. Overview

Nouns name people, places, things, or ideas. There are proper nouns and common nouns.

Proper noun: **George** [Name]

Common noun: **girl** [how discribe]

B. Proper Nouns

1. Proper nouns are names of **particular** people, places, things, and ideas.

   People: **Mary Larson**

   Places: **France**

   Things and ideas: **the Empire State Building** (buildings), **Saturday** (days of the week), **May** (months of the year), **Arabic** (languages), **British** (nationalities), **Christmas** (holidays)

2. A proper noun always begins with a capital letter.

   British
     NOT: ~~british~~

   Saturday
     NOT: ~~saturday~~

3. *A/An* is not usually used with proper nouns. But some proper nouns begin with *the*.

   the *New York Times*

   the Five Spice Restaurant

   the Middle East

C. Common Nouns

1. All other nouns are common nouns. They do not name particular people, places, things, or ideas.

   girl, **cat**, **car**

2. A common noun does not usually begin with a capital letter unless it is the first word in a sentence.

   Henry Ford invented the **automobile**.

   Automobiles are very common today.

3. *A/An* can be used with singular common nouns. *The* can be used with singular and plural common nouns.

   (See Grammar Briefing 2 in this chapter for more information about singular and plural nouns.)

   He invented **a machine**.

   It was **an invention** with many problems.

   The machine didn't work well.

   None of **the machines** worked well.

GRAMMAR **HOT**SPOT!

The days of the week and the months of the year are proper nouns. The seasons of the year are common nouns. They do not begin with a capital letter.

He came on a **Sunday** in the **fall**.

NOT: He came on a **Sunday** in the ~~Fall~~.

GRAMMAR PRACTICE 1

Proper Nouns and Common Nouns

1 **Proper and Common Nouns:** Those Magnificent Men and Their Flying Machines

A. Listen to a museum guide talk about the history of flight. He describes six different flying machines. Put these machines in the order in which you hear them: 1 = the first; 6 = the last.

_____ the *Type XI*

_____ duck-foot wings

1 _____ ornithopter

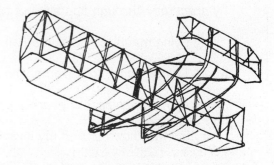

_____ the *Flyer III*

_____ the *Flyer*

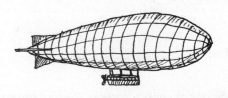

_____ a hydrogen balloon

B. Look at the chart about some of the inventors from Part A. Correct the errors. There are 20 errors with capital letters. The first two are corrected for you.

Who	When	Where
a ~~f~~French man, ~~b~~Besnier	1678	France
~~j~~Jacques ~~c~~Charles	the Winter of 1783	France
The ~~o~~Orville and ~~w~~Wilbur ~~w~~Wright	~~t~~Thursday, ~~d~~December 17, 1903—just before ~~c~~Christmas	the ~~u~~United ~~s~~States
~~t~~The ~~w~~Wright ~~b~~Brothers	1905	the ~~u~~United ~~s~~States
~~l~~Louis ~~b~~Bleriot	1908	the ~~e~~English ~~c~~Channel

2 Editing: Proper and Common Nouns—Come Fly with Me

A. An inventor living in New York in 1903 is writing to his girlfriend. Correct the errors in his letter. There are eight errors with common nouns and proper nouns. The first two are corrected for you.

Dear ~~a~~ Gloria,   July 14, 1903

Hello from ~~the~~ New York! I miss you, but I will see you soon. You see, my invention is almost ready. It is a beautiful flying machine. I will name it gloria, for you. It will fly gracefully through the air and take me to the Paris; I will meet you there.

My flying machine has three pairs of Wings. These wings are made of heavy wood. I glued them to a frame. The frame is very strong. I will sit in the center of my flying machine. I will turn a pedals with my Feet and it will move forward. Everyone will know me and my invention. And you and I will spend the Winter together, traveling around in my flying machine. We will be famous.

I can't wait to see you, my darling. Look for me in the sky!

Love,

Dick

Dick

B. Work with a partner. Discuss: Do you think Dick's invention was a success? Why or why not?

Count and Noncount Nouns

FORM and FUNCTION

A. Count Nouns

1. Count nouns are names for people, places, things, and ideas that can be counted. There can be one (singular) or more than one (plural).

   Singular: a **girl**, one **child**
   Plural: two **girls**, five **children**

2. All regular plural count nouns end in *-s.*

   (See Appendix 8 for spelling rules for plural nouns.)

   books, dogs, bushes

3. The regular plural ending is pronounced /s/, /z/, or /ɪz/.

   (See Appendix 9 for the pronounciation rules for plural nouns.)

   /**s**/: books
   /**z**/: books
   /**ɪz**/: books

4. Some count nouns have irregular plural forms.

   (See Appendix 10 for a list of common irregular plural nouns.)

SINGULAR	PLURAL
child	**children**
foot	**feet**
woman	**women**
sheep	**sheep**
person	**people**

B. Noncount Nouns

1. Noncount nouns (sometimes called mass nouns or uncountable nouns) are names for people, places, things, and ideas that cannot be counted.

   water, information, air, beauty

2. A noncount noun does not have a plural form.

   homework
     NOT: ~~homeworks~~

   information
     NOT: ~~informations~~

3. Many noncount nouns name groups of things. These groups have individual countable parts.

GROUPS (NONCOUNT NOUNS)	INDIVIDUAL PARTS (COUNT NOUNS)
homework	writing assignments, math problems
jewelry	a bracelet, earrings
luggage	a suitcase, bags
equipment	a hair dryer, computers
clothing	a sweater, socks

(continued on next page)

4. Other categories of noncount nouns include:

LIQUIDS	SOLIDS	PARTICLES	GASES	NATURAL PHENOMENA	ABSTRACT IDEAS	FIELDS OF STUDY
milk	food	sand	air	weather	honesty	journalism
water	hair	sugar	hydrogen	scenery	beauty	mathematics

(See Appendix 11 for a list of common noncount nouns.)

GRAMMAR **HOT**SPOT!

1. Singular count nouns and noncount nouns take singular verbs.

                 singular   singular
                 noun   verb
The   **boy**   **is**   tired.

noncount   singular
noun   verb
Sugar   **is**   sweet.

2. Plural count nouns take plural verbs.

    plural   plural
    noun   verb
The **boys**   **are**   tired.

3. Some noncount nouns end in -s. These nouns look plural, but they are not.

The **news** on television is usually bad.
  NOT: The news on television ~~are~~ usually bad.

Mathematics is difficult.
  NOT: Mathematics ~~are~~ difficult.

Count and Noncount Nouns

3 Singular and Plural Count Nouns: What Happened to Amelia Earhart?

Imagine it is the year 1937. Listen to the news report about Amelia Earhart, a famous woman pilot. Complete the report with the words you hear. Write the correct form of the nouns in parentheses: singular or plural. See Appendix 8 and Appendix 10 for help.

. . . We interrupt this program to bring you some sad news. Amelia Earhart, world-famous pilot, is lost. Earhart and her copilot, Fred Noonan, were almost at the end of their **flight** 1 (flight) around the world. Yesterday, however, they tried to land on Howland Island, a small **island** 2 (island) in the Pacific Ocean. But something went wrong. The **men** 3 (man) on a nearby **ship** 4 (ship) lost contact with them early yesterday morning.

Many **people** 5 (person) are looking for Earhart and Noonan. Even small **children** 6 (child) from other **islandes** 7 (island) are helping. Young **boys** 8 (boy) from New Guinea are looking in the **bush** 9 (bush) on Howland Island for airplane **parts** 10 (part). We need to find Earhart and Noonan soon. They didn't have many **supplies** 11 (supply) on their plane. There are **fish** 12 (fish) in the **water** 13 (water) near Howland Island, and there are wild **berries** 14 (berry) on the island. But these two **heroes** 15 (hero) will not live long without help. Keep your **radios** 16 (radio) tuned to this station for more information.

bush = short treelike plant. *supply* = something (food, water, etc.) people need to survive. *berry* = small juicy fruit. *hero* = person of great courage.

4. Pronunciation of Plural Nouns: More About Amelia Earhart

A. The year is now 2004. The search for Amelia Earhart continues. Listen to part of a television show about her. Above each **boldfaced** noun, write the plural sound you hear: /s/ (as in *hats*), /z/ (as in *dogs*), or /ɪz/ as in *dishes*.

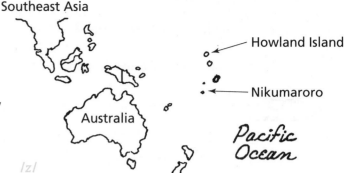

Southeast Asia

Howland Island

Nikumaroro

Australia

Pacific Ocean

/z/
Amelia Earhart disappeared almost 70 **years** ago.
                                          1

What happened to Amelia and her airplane, the *Electra*?

Did they fall into the sea near Howland Island? Many **books** are written about this
                                                        2
theory. There are, however, other **theories**. Tonight's program is
                                    3
about a new theory.

This year, **researchers** found some interesting **objects** on another island, Nikumaroro
             4   5
Island. This island is 350 **miles** from Howland Island. They found **pieces** of **shoes**.
                            6   7   8
Amelia Earhart wore shoes just like these. In other **places** on Nikumaroro Island,
                                                     9
searchers also found old airplane **parts.** Are some of them from the *Electra*?
                                   10

Many people now believe Amelia Earhart landed on Nikumaroro Island. Others

disagree. They tell us airplane **crashes** were very common in 1937. They believe the
                                 11
objects from Nikumaroro probably belonged to someone else. They say Earhart and

Noonan did not have enough fuel in their **tanks** to reach Nikumaroro. Radio **records**
                                         12   13
also tell us the *Electra* was flying very close to Howland Island when it crashed.

So what really happened to Amelia Earhart? In this week's television program, we will

show you **photographs** and **maps.** We will give you more **details**. Then you can decide!
          14   15   16
We will be right back. But, first, these **messages** . . .
                                        17

> *theory* = belief. *researcher* = person who does careful study. *crash* = accident.
> *tank* = container for holding gasoline. *record* = written account that saves knowledge.

B. Read the news report aloud to a partner. Help each other pronounce the plural nouns correctly.

C. What happened to Amelia Earhart? With your partner, write your own ending to her story. Use one of the theories from Exercise 3 or Exercise 4, or use your imagination! Write at least seven sentences. Read your ending to the class. Be careful about your pronunciation of plurals. See the spelling and pronunciation rules in Appendix 8 and Appendix 9 for help.

See the *Grammar Links* Website for more about the mystery of Amelia Earhart.

5 Regular and Irregular Plural Nouns: Time for a Race

A. How many plural nouns can you think of? Divide into two teams and stand in two lines. The first person in each team writes a different **regular** plural noun on the blackboard and runs to the end of the line. The next person writes a different regular plural noun. Continue the game until one team can't think of any more nouns or for 10 minutes.

B. Now play the same game with **irregular** plural nouns.

6 Singular, Plural, and Noncount Nouns: Modern Airplane Travelers

Read the story. Write each **boldfaced** noun in the correct column of the chart.

Jack and Jill are **students** at the University of Maine, where there is a lot of **snow** during the winter **months**. Jack studies **mathematics**, and Jill studies **journalism**.

Jack and Jill work very hard, and they usually have a lot of **homework** every night. But tonight Jack and Jill are not thinking about homework. They're busy planning a **vacation** instead.

Next **week** is winter vacation week at the University of Maine. Jack and Jill are tired of the cold Maine **weather**, so they're going to take a **trip** to California. They'll visit Jill's **sister**, **brother**, and **cousins** there. While they're in California, Jack and Jill will also go to the **beach**. They'll lie on the **sand**. They'll swim in the warm **water** of the southern Pacific Ocean. They'll breathe the sweet salt **air**. They'll eat **seafood**. They'll watch the **whales** and the **fish** in the sea. They'll enjoy the **beauty** of the landscape. They'll just—relax.

Count and Noncount Nouns		
Singular Count Nouns	Plural Count Nouns	Noncount Nouns
	students	

A. Jack and Jill are deciding what to take on their vacation. They are making lists. Put the items from their lists into the categories in the chart. Some items won't fit any of the categories. Put them in the box marked Other.

Jill's list

gold earrings
bikini
backpack for the beach
journalism assignment
3 cotton dresses
Jack's CD player
shampoo
new watch
makeup
toothbrush

Shaver

Jack's list

large suitcase—for both of us

laptop computer

swimsuit

soap

3 pairs of shorts

electric shaver

math problems

surprise gift for Jill—necklace

toothpaste

toothbrush

Shorts

Bikini

	Groups (Noncount)				
	Homework	Jewelry	Luggage	Electronic Equipment	Clothing
Individual Items (Count)		gold earrings			

Other
makeup NC

B. Look at the nouns you put in the *Other* box. Label each noun **SC** (Singular Count), **PC** (Plural Count), or **NC** (Noncount). Not sure whether a noun is count or noncount? Look it up in your dictionary.

8 **Verb Agreement with Count and Noncount Nouns:** Taxi, Please!

Read the passage. Circle the correct verb forms.

The first airplane flight was only about 50 years ago, but people (is / are) already flying

to the moon! Space travel (is / are) becoming common, but it is difficult, too. Space (has / have)

no gravity. In space, humans (weighs / weight) almost nothing. Weightlessness (makes / make)

it difficult to work and to eat. Food (floats / float) away when you try to eat it, and tools

(becomes / become) difficult to use. Nowadays, special new tools (helps / help) astronauts

work in weightlessness; special food (is / are) also available.

Temperature (is / are) another problem in space. Outer space (is / are) very cold
                     10   11
in some places and very hot in others. Space suits (protects / protect) astronauts from
                                                         12
freezing or burning in space.

Even with these problems, people still (wants / want) to travel in space. In fact, one
                                                  13
company (is / are) building space "taxis." These taxis (is / are) waiting to take us to the
            14   15
moon someday soon! Are you ready to go? Just pack your space suit and call your local

space taxi for a ride!

---

gravity = the natural force that pulls toward the center of the earth. *weightlessness* = the condition
of having no weight. astronaut = a person who travels in space.

GRAMMAR BRIEFING 3

The Indefinite Article A/An → A/An

FORM

A. Overview

A/An is the indefinite article. *A/An* comes before singular counts nouns.	**a** boy **an** apple

B. *A* or *An*?

1. Use *a* before consonant sounds. Use *an* before vowel sounds.	**a** baby, **a** class **an** island, **an** orange
2. Vowel letters do not always have vowel sounds.	**an** uncle BUT: **a** university
3. Some words that begin with the consonant letter *h* begin with vowel sounds.	**a** horse BUT: **an** hour

(continued on next page)

Introducing Nouns

1. *A/An* introduces singular count nouns. A noun needs to be introduced when:

Speaker   Listener

- The speaker knows about it but the listener does not.

Speaker: I saw **a** cool car today.

Speaker   Listener

- The listener knows about it but the speaker does not.

Speaker: I hear you bought **a** new car today. What did you buy?

Speaker   Listener

- It is new for both the listener and the speaker.

Speaker: I need **a** new car. What kind should I get?

2. Don't use an article when noncount nouns and plural nouns need to be introduced.

I'm going to buy **bread** today. (noncount noun)

I need **shoes**. (plural count noun)

The Indefinite Article *A/An*

9 The Indefinite Article: A Car for Christine

Christine and Roger are talking on the telephone. Complete their conversation with *a* or *an*. Write **0** when no article is needed.

Christine: I really need ___*a*___ new car.
1

Roger: Oh, yeah? What kind are you looking for?

Christine: Oh, I don't know. I just need _____an_____ inexpensive, dependable car.
2

Roger: Well, I just bought _____an_____ used car.
3

Christine: What kind did you buy?

Roger: It's _____an_____ orange sports car. It needs _____an_____
4   5

tires, but it's in good shape.

Christine: You're lucky!

Roger: Hey! I saw _____an_____ interesting car the other day. You might like it.
6

Christine: Really? Where?

Roger: It was at _____a_____ house in Williston.
7

Christine: Well, that's pretty far from my apartment . . .

Roger: You have _____an_____ apartment downtown, right?
8

Christine: Yeah. That's right. It's on Spear Street.

Roger: Do you have _____a_____ time right now? Do you want to look at
9

_____a_____ cars?
10

Christine: Well, I guess so. I have _____a_____ homework to do, but—
11

Roger: Great! I'll come and pick you up in my new car.

Christine: Okay. Let's see. You'll probably be here in about _____a_____ hour, right?
12

Roger: Are you kidding? Not in my new beauty! See you in 30 minutes!

Christine: Okay, Roger. But do drive carefully. Roger? Are you there?

The Definite Article *The*

FORM and FUNCTION

A. Overview

The is the definite article. It comes before singular, plural, and noncount nouns.	**the** boy (singular) **the** boys (plural) **the** sugar (noncount)

B. When to Use *The*

Use *the* only when the speaker and the listener are thinking about the same noun.
Both the speaker and the listener know about the noun. This happens:

• The second time someone mentions a noun.	I have a car and a truck. **The** car is new. **The** truck is old. (*Car* and *truck* are introduced with *a*; the second time they are mentioned, *the* is used.)
• When the noun is part of or related to something else already introduced.	I bought a new car yesterday. **The** seats are leather. (We know which seats, since seats are part of the car.)
• When the noun names something unique (one of a kind). There is only one of this person, place, or thing in the world.	**The** sun was hot today. (There is only one sun, and everyone knows about it.)
• When the noun is part of the everyday world of the listener and the speaker. It is something or someone that is very familiar to them.	*Mother to son*: Did you wash **the** dishes? (The dishes are part of their house; mother and son both know these dishes.) *Friend to friend*: I was listening to **the** news on **the** radio this morning when **the** electricity went off. (The news, the radio, and the electricity are parts of everyday life; it is not necessary to introduce them.)
• When other words in the sentence make the noun known (specific).	**The** book **on the table** is mine. (*On the table* tells which book.) **The second** book was the best. (*Second* tells which book.)
• When the listener and speaker can see or hear the noun (or the speaker points to the noun).	Did you hear **the** thunder? (The speaker and listener hear the thunder.) Carol, give me **the** book, please. (The speaker is pointing at the book.)

The Definite Article *The*

10 The Definite Article: The Age of Automobiles

Read this passage from a history book. Above each **boldfaced** phrase, write the letter of the reason why *the* is used. Choose from the reasons in the box.

> A. The noun has already been introduced.
> B. The noun is part of something else already introduced.
> C. The noun is unique. There is only one of this noun.
> D. Other words in the sentence make the noun known (specific).

Henry Ford was born in 1863 on a farm in Michigan. **The farm** belonged to his parents,
(A) — 1

William and Mary Ford. Ford worked hard on **the farm**, and he went to school in a one-room schoolhouse.
(B) — 2

The schoolhouse was small and crowded, and he didn't like it very much. So when he was 16 years old,
(C) — 3

Ford left home. He went to Detroit and found a job in a machine shop. In **the machine shop**, Ford
(D) — 4

learned a lot about engines. **The men** around Ford admired him. He worked very hard. When **the sun**
(B) — 5   *(C) — 6*

rose in the morning, Henry was already working. When **the moon** rose at night, Henry was still working.
(C) — 7

While he was working in the machine shop, Ford decided to build a new kind of machine—an

automobile. His first automobile was the "Quadricycle." The Quadricycle was an interesting car. **The frame**
(D) — 8

was metal. **The wheels** were bicycle wheels. People liked the Quadricycle, but it was very expensive.
(D) — 9

In 1908, Ford introduced his Model T. Then, in 1913, he started **the first assembly line**.
(C) — 10

With **the assembly line**, he produced many cars at one time. In this way, many Model T's
(A) — 11

were made at the same time and at a low cost. **The car** was not expensive,
(D) — 12

and people all over **the world** began to use it. This was the beginning of
(C) — 13

the Age of Automobiles.

Quadricycle

> *machine shop* = a place where machines are made. *engine* = the part of a car
> that changes energy into motion. *frame* = the inside structure of a car.
> *assembly line* = machines and workers in a factory that work together.

 See the *Grammar Links* Website for more about the history of the automobile.

11 The Definite Article: A Sunday Drive

Henry and Clara are going for a ride in their Model T. Read their conversation. Above each **boldfaced** phrase, write the letter of the reason why *the* is used. Choose from the reasons in the box.

> A. The person, place, or thing is unique. There is only one in the world.
> B. The person, place, or thing is part of Henry and Clara's everyday world.
> C. Henry and Clara can see or hear the person, place, or thing.

Henry: Clara, are you ready? We need to leave soon, or **the sun** will go down.
       (A) 1

Clara: I'm almost ready. But before we go, we need to feed **the cats**. And did you put
       (B) 2

      the dog outside?
       (B) 3

Henry: Yes, I did. Now can we go?

Clara: Well, just a minute. I need to . . . Did you see that? **The lightning** is getting close!
       (A) 4

      I heard on **the radio** this morning that **the weather** is going to be bad this afternoon.
       (B) 5   *(C)* 6

Henry: But look at **the clouds**. They are very far away. It isn't going to rain here. And
       (A) 7

      rain won't bother us anyway. **The car** has a top on it. We won't get wet! I'll go
       (B) 8

      outside and get **the car** ready.
       (B) 9

Clara: Well, just in case, I'm going to bring **the umbrella**. Oh, Henry! Did you hear
       (C) 10

      that? **The thunder** is really loud now!
       (C) 11

Henry: That wasn't thunder, Clara. The car sometimes makes a little noise when I first

      start it. Let's go!

Definite and Indefinite Articles: Test Yourself

Complete the sentences with *a, an,* or *the.* If no article is needed, write **0**.

1. We have _a_ black cat, _a_ gray cat, and _an_ orange cat. _The_ black cat and _the_ orange cat are friendly. _The_ gray cat is very independent. We love _0_ cats.

2. Yesterday I bought _X_ furniture. I bought _a_ new couch and two new armchairs. _a_ couch is purple. _an_ armchairs are green.

3. Carlos is _the_ very nice man. He brought us _____ flowers when he came to visit.

4. Last week Wan met _the_ president of his country. It was _X_ honor.

5. We need _X_ milk. _the_ milk in our refrigerator is sour.

6. Andrew and Clarice are cleaning their house this weekend. It will be _a_ _X_ big job. They want to wash all _X_ windows, reorganize all _____ closets, and shampoo all _X_ carpets.

7. Answer _____ door, please. _the_ doorbell is ringing.

8. There are _____ apples in the bowl. Do you want one?

9. Do you hear _a_ rain? It is falling softly on _the_ roof.

10. I need _an_ information about _the_ price of this car.

11. _the_ mayor is going to make _a_ speech tonight at 9:00. She's going to talk about our city. Let's listen to _the_ radio at that time.

12. Karen recently had _an_ unpleasant experience. She applied to _an_ university in California. There are several universities there, but she applied to only one. _the_ university didn't accept her.

13 **Understanding Situations: Listening In**

A. You are in a crowded airport. You hear the following conversations. Write about the conversations. Make guesses: Who are the two people? What are the people talking about? Use your imagination. Pay special attention to your use of definite and indefinite articles.

1. Two young girls are talking. One says to the other: "Do you think she remembered **the bag**?"

   Example:

   The two girls are sisters. The bag is a bag of toys. They want their mother to bring the bag with the toys on the airplane. OR The two girls are friends. They are waiting for another girl to join them. She has their concert tickets in a bag.

2. Two older women are coming out of an airplane. One says to the other: "Did you remember **the oranges**?"

3. A man is greeting a woman. He says to her: "Welcome home! Did you get **the job**?"

4. Two women are walking near you. One says to the other: "I have **the tickets** right here."

5. Two young boys are looking around. One says to the other: "Where's the rest of **the team**?"

6. Two college students sit next to you. One says to the other: "Where's **the computer**?"

B. Exchange papers with a partner. Read your partner's answers. Discuss: Which of your answers are similar? Which are different?

See the *Grammar Links* Website for model answers to this exercise.

Check your progress! Go to the Self-Test for Chapter 8 on the *Grammar Links* Website.

Chapter 9

General Quantifiers; Numbers; Measure Words

Introductory Task: Seeing It All!

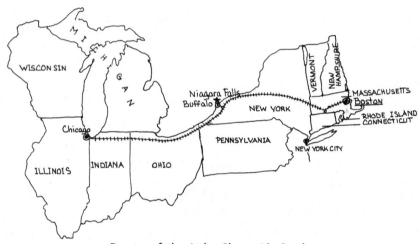

Route of the Lake Shore Limited

🎧 **A.** Kim and Juan are planning a vacation trip together. Listen to their conversation, and write the words you hear.

Kim: Niagara Falls! Boston! New York! I want to see ___all___ these places! And I want to visit

___some___ small towns and see ___some___ scenery, too!

     2   3

Juan: Wait. I have an idea. There's a train from Chicago. It goes to Boston and New York.

It's called the Lake Shore Limited. We can buy a ticket to Boston, but we can visit

_____ other places, too. For example, we can stop and visit
          4

Niagara Falls. Then, _____ days later, we can get back on the train.
                    5

The train passes by _____ beautiful scenery, and it stops at
                      6

_____ small towns, too. What do you think?
      7

Kim: Interesting idea. But train travel takes _____ time, and there isn't
8

_____ space on trains.
9

Juan: Well, the Lake Shore Limited is different! It's a fast train. And travel on this train is really

quite comfortable. For example, for _____ extra money, you can
10

get a "sleeper." _____ sleeper is a room with a large bed and
11

_____ windows. _____ sleepers even have
12   13

televisions in them! And _____ passengers in sleepers eat for free
14

in the dining car. _____ food is fresh, and _____
15   16

table has fresh flowers on it.

Kim: That does sound nice! Maybe the train is a good idea, after all. Let's get

_____ information about schedules and prices.
17

See the *Grammar Links* Website for more information about traveling by train in the
United States.

B. Look again at the words you wrote in Part A. These words are general quantifiers.
Write them in the correct columns in the chart. Are you unsure which nouns are
count and which are noncount? See Grammar Briefing 2 in Chapter 8, or look them
up in your dictionary.

Quantifiers used before **singular count** nouns	Quantifiers used before **plural count** nouns	Quantifiers used before **noncount** noun
	all some	

C. Look at the quantifiers you wrote in Part B. Find the ones that are used with both
plural count and noncount nouns. Write them here:

_____

General Quantifiers I

FORM and FUNCTION

A. Overview

General quantifiers express different quantities (amount of something, number of something). Some general quantifiers can be used only with plural count nouns. Others can be used only with noncount nouns. Some can be used with both.

	WITH PLURAL COUNT NOUNS	WITH NONCOUNT NOUNS	WITH BOTH
largest quantity			**all**
			most
	many	**much**	**a lot (of), lots (of)**
	several	**a great deal (of)**	
			enough, plenty (of)
			some
	a few	**a little**	
	few	**little**	
no quantity			**none (of the), no**

B. *Each* and *Every*

Use *each* and *every* only with singular count nouns. They take singular verbs. They mean "all."

Each/Every train on this route **has** a sleeping car. = **All** trains on this route **have** sleeping cars.

GRAMMAR PRACTICE 1

General Quantifiers I

1 **General Quantifiers with Count and Noncount Nouns:** Train Talk

Cross out the general quantifiers that *cannot* be used to complete the sentence correctly.

1. This city has _____ train stations.

a few	many
~~a little~~	enough
~~each~~	few
a lot of	lots of
no	plenty of
~~a great deal of~~	

2. Peter has _____ baggage.

a few	many
a little	enough
each	few
a lot of	lots of
no	plenty of
a great deal of	

3. _____ large cities have trains.

Most	Every
Few	Much
Several	Some
Little	A lot of
All	

4. _____ travel by trains takes place during the summer.

Most	Every
Few	Much
Several	Some
Little	A lot of
All	

2 General Quantifiers—Form and Meaning: Railroads

A. Read the passage. Circle the correct quantifiers.

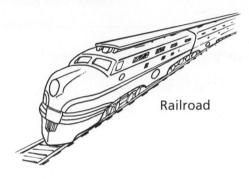

Railroad

Mobile Home

Trains are very common. They are found in almost (no / (every)) country of the
world. Trains roll on tracks. (Each / All) tracks are made of long pieces of steel,
called rails. When (several / no) rails join together, they make a "road" of rails—
a railroad. There are more than 14 million miles of railroad in the world. Railroads
carry people and things to (few / many) different places.

In the 1800s, travel by train was very popular in the United States. (Many / few)
people traveled by train. In the early 1900s, however, (lots of / much) people began
to buy cars. Train companies began to lose money. (Several / Little) years later, the
mobile home became popular. People pulled these "homes away from home" behind
their cars. (All / A little) mobile homes had beds in them, so they made travel private,
comfortable, and inexpensive.

Finally, airplane travel became inexpensive and more popular. (No / Most) people
preferred air travel over train travel. By the mid-1960s, passenger trains almost
completely disappeared. There were (many / much) other easy ways to travel in
the United States.

B. Write the correct quantifiers on the lines.

Today, _____ people are riding trains again. There are now new
                    1 (a few / little)

trains with extra services. _____ passenger can now eat and sleep
                              2 (Every / All)

comfortably on the train. _____ long-distance train tries to serve
                            3 (Each / All)

elegant food in its dining car. _____ long-distance trains also have
                                  4 (Most / Much)

sleeping cars with bathrooms and comfortable beds in them. _____
                                                            5 (Some / None)

sleeping cars have television sets and telephones. There are now _____
                                                                  6 (several / a great deal of)

types of tickets for train travelers. There are _____ inexpensive
                                                  7 (few of / plenty of)

tickets on scenic routes. Will passenger trains become popular again? Are there going to be

_____ passengers now? Only time will tell.
8 (enough / a great deal of)

General Quantifiers II

FORM

A. More About *Much* and *Many*

1. Remember! Use *much* with noncount nouns. Use *many* with count nouns. (See Grammar Briefing 1.)

   We don't have **much** time.
   We don't have **many** books.

2. Use *how much* to ask about noncount nouns. Use *how many* to ask about count nouns.

   How much money do you have?
   How many books do you have?

3. *Many* is common in affirmative and negative statements and in questions.

   I have **many** books.
   I don't have **many** books.
   How **many** books do you have?

4. *Much* is common in questions and negative statements. In affirmative statements, use another quantifier with a similar meaning, such as *lots of* or *a lot of.*

   I don't have **much** free time.
   How **much** free time do you have?
   I have **a lot of/plenty of** free time.
     NOT: I have ~~much~~ free time.

(continued on next page)

B. More About *Some* and *Any*

1. Use *some* in affirmative statements with count and noncount nouns.

   I have **some** cats.

   I have **some** time.

2. Use *any* in most negative statements and questions.

   I don't have **any** dogs.

   Do you have **any** dogs?

FUNCTION

A. *Too Much* and *Too Many*

Too much and *too many* have a negative meaning. They describe a quantity that is more than it should be.

She ate **too much** cake. She was sick.

They bought **too many** new plants. They had no place to put them.

B. *Few* and *Little*; *A Few* and *A Little*

1. *Few* and *little* usually mean "almost no" or "not enough."

   I'm not happy here. I have **few** friends, and I never go out. (not enough friends)

   Hurry! There's very **little** time before the train leaves. (almost no time)

2. *A few* and *a little* mean "a small quantity" or "not a lot, but enough." (*A lot > a little/ a few > very little/very few > none.*)

   I'm happy here. I have **a few** friends, and we go out often. (not a lot of friends, but enough)

   Relax. We have **a little** time before the train leaves. (not a lot of time, but enough)

C. *Enough* and *Plenty* (*Of*)

1. *Enough* and *plenty* (*of*) have similar meanings. *Enough* means "a good quantity, what you need." *Plenty* (*of*) means "enough" or "a little more than enough."

   A: Would you like more dessert?

   B: No, thanks. I've had **enough/plenty of** sweets for one day!

GRAMMAR HOTSPOT!

General quantifiers usually occur with nouns. However (except for *no* and *every*), they can also be used alone when their meaning is clear.

Customer: I'd like a ticket, please.

Ticket agent: Sorry. We don't have **any** tickets.
OR Sorry. We don't have **any**.
NOT: Sorry. ~~We have **no**.~~

GRAMMAR PRACTICE 2

General Quantifiers II

3 *Some* and *Any*; *Too Much* and *Too Many*; *A Lot of* and *Lots of*:
Wonder of the World!

Complete Kim's travel journal with the correct quantifiers.

This week we are really having __a lot of__ fun. We're riding the Lake Shore Limited
1 (much / a lot of)
to _____ different places.
2 (lots of / too many)

Our first stop was Niagara Falls. We spent _____ time there because it
3 (lots of / much)
was so beautiful. It is one of the Seven Wonders of the World. _____
4 (Lots of / Much)
water pours over the edge of Niagara Falls—almost 400,000 tons a minute! When the tour guide
told us this, I thought he was wrong. 400,000 tons sounded like _____. But
5 (too much / much)
when I saw Niagara Falls, I changed my mind. The falls are huge! _____ people
6 (Too many / Lots of)
come to see and hear them.

We didn't have _____ trouble with the weather at Niagara Falls.
7 (some / any)
There was _____ sunshine every day. But we got very wet anyway! Why?
8 (some / any)
Well, when the water falls over the edge, it fills the air with _____
9 (much / lots of)
mist. There's also _____ wind near the falls, and the wind blows mist
10 (a lot of / much)
everywhere! _____ people don't like this. They say there is
11 (Some / Any)
_____ mist; but I disagree. I love the mist; it makes beautiful rainbows.
12 (too much / much)

We didn't spend _____ money at Niagara Falls, but I think maybe we
13 (too much / some)
took _____ pictures. Over 100! We won't have _____
14 (many / too many)   15 (some / any)
film left for other things, and we have _____ more places to visit.
16 (some / any)

4 *Few, A Few, Little,* and *A Little*: Riding the Rails

Complete the sentences with *few, a few, little,* or *a little.*

1. Kim and Juan have __little_____ time before their train leaves. They're worried. They might miss it!

2. Kim has _____ extra money. He's happy. He's going to buy another postcard.

3. Kim has very _____ friends in the United States. He hopes to meet new people on the train.

4. Juan has _____ friends in the United States. He'll send them postcards from the next stop.

5. Kim and Juan want to stop for five days in New York at the end of their trip. They can do that because they will have _____ vacation time left.

6. Kim and Juan are planning to visit the mountains of Massachusetts. It is very peaceful in these mountains. There is _____ traffic, and there are _____ crimes.

7. Kim's seat is broken. He says to the conductor, "Excuse me. I'm having _____ problems with my seat."

8. Kim has very _____ money left at the end of the trip. He doesn't buy any gifts.

5 General Quantifiers—Form and Meaning: A Difficult Choice

A. Look at the pictures. What do you think of each vacation? Complete the descriptions with the quantifiers in the box. (More than one answer is possible.)

a lot of/lots of	a few
too many	a little
enough	plenty (of)
too much	no
little	few
a great deal of	

New York

Rustic Retreat

New York		Rustic Retreat	
plenty of	museums	_no_	museums
OR			
too many	museums		
	peace and quiet		peace and quiet
	traffic		traffic
	nightlife		nightlife
	people		people
	nature hikes		nature hikes
	theaters		theaters
	wild animals		wild animals
	interesting scenery		interesting scenery

B. Work with a partner. Ask and answer questions about New York and the Rustic Retreat. Use general quantifiers with nouns and general quantifiers without nouns in your answers. Do you and your partner agree? Discuss.

Examples: Question: How many museums are there in New York?
Possible Answers: Too many! OR It has too many museums!
Question: Does the Rustic Retreat have any museums?
Possible Answers: No, it doesn't have any. OR No, it doesn't have any museums. OR No, none.

C. Imagine you are riding the train. You can stop either in New York or at the Rustic Retreat. Which one do you choose? Write a paragraph of at least five sentences about your choice. Use general quantifiers.

Example: I choose the Rustic Retreat. Every activity there is relaxing. It has a lot of beautiful scenery. . . .

See the *Grammar Links* Website for a complete model paragraph for this assignment.

6 General Quantifiers—The Good and the Bad

A. Choose one of the pairs of topics below. In the chart on page 166, write two sentences about the good things and two sentences about the bad things about your topic. In each sentence, use a general quantifier from the box. Use a different quantifier in each sentence.

1. A. travel on foot
   B. travel by car

2. A. ski vacation
   B. beach vacation

3. A. travel by plane
   B. travel by train

4. A. vacation alone
   B. vacation with friends

all	most
each	(too) much
enough	none
every	plenty (of)
(too) many	some
several	a great deal of

Example:

A. SKI VACATION	
Good	**Bad**
I spend many warm evenings by the fire. There's plenty of snow.	It's cold every day. There isn't much sun.
B. BEACH VACATION	
Good	**Bad**
I have enough time to read a good book. All beach sunsets are beautiful.	Some beaches are dirty. I get too much sand in my hair.

A.

Good	**Bad**

B.

Good	**Bad**

B. Discuss your chart in Part A with the rest of the class. Make a class list. What is good and what is bad about each topic?

Numbers and Measure Words

FORM and FUNCTION

A. Numbers

We use definite numbers (*one, two, three, four, five*, etc.) to count people, places, and things. The patterns are: • *One* + singular count noun. • All other numbers + plural noun.	**one** book, **two** books, **three** books

B. Measure Words

Measure words express specific or exact (not general) amounts. Most measure words follow this pattern:

A/ONE/TWO THREE, ETC.	MEASURE WORD	OF	PLURAL COUNT NOUN
a	box		paper clips
a	cup	of	beans
two	pounds		apples

			NONCOUNT NOUN
a	box		paper
a	cup	of	sugar
two	pounds		meat

C. Special Measure Words

Certain nouns have special measure words. These measure words are used only with a small group of nouns.	a **bunch** of grapes, a **bunch** of bananas a **clove** of garlic a **head** of lettuce, a **head** of cauliflower a **loaf** of bread

GRAMMAR **HOT**SPOT!

1. Do not use *of* after definite numbers.

> We live ten miles from town.
> **NOT:** We live ten ~~of~~ miles from town.

2. Do not add a plural *-s* to definite numbers.

> We live ten miles from town.
> **NOT:** We live ten~~s~~ miles from town.

TALKING THE TALK

In speaking, the *f* sound in the word *of* in quantifiers and measure words is often dropped.

WRITING	SPEAKING
Joe has **a lot of** friends.	Joe has **a lotta** friends.
This recipe needs **four cups of** water.	This recipe needs **four cupsa** water.

GRAMMAR PRACTICE 3

Numbers and Measure Words

7   **Numbers and Measure Words:** Home Away from Home I

Dick York is a retired English professor. He is giving a talk to other retired people about traveling. Read and listen to the first part of Dick's talk. Circle the numbers and measure words that you hear.

Hello, fellow travelers! As you know, my wife, Helen, and I travel a lot. We used

to travel by train, but then we discovered campers—mobile homes—and we just love

them! We travel (10,000 / 10,000 of) miles a year in our mobile home. Sometimes
                                    1

we drive (600 / 600 of) miles a day. Sometimes we cover only (60 / 60 of).
          2   3

Today I'm going to talk about traveling in a mobile home. What do you need to

take with you? Of course you'll need (a /one of) good road map, but there are a few
                                        4

other items you need as well. Always take (two / two of) extra tires. It's no fun
                                            5

having a flat tire (50 of / 50) miles from a city. Make sure you also take at least
                    6

(five extra gallons / five extra gallon of) gasoline. I always take (a quart / a quart of) oil, too.
        7   8

168   Unit Four   Nouns, Articles, Quantifiers, and Pronouns

You'll also need a good first-aid kit in your mobile home.

Make sure you have (box of / a box of) bandages,
9

(a can / a can of) insect repellent, (a bottle / a bottle of)
10   11

rubbing alcohol, and (a jar / a jar of) first-aid cream.
12

Bandage

First-Aid Cream

8 Numbers and Measure Words: Home Away from Home II

Listen to more advice about mobile home travel. Write the words you hear.
Use the words in the box in this pattern: *a/one/two/three, etc.* + measure word
from the box + *of.*

bag	box	carton	pound	small basket	✓tube
bar	bunch	couple	quart	stick	
bottle	can	head	roll	tin	

1. _a tube of_ _____ toothpaste
2. _____ soap
3. _____ shampoo
4. _____ toilet tissue
5. _____ milk
6. _____ butter
7. _____ eggs
8. _____ lettuce
9. _____ meat
10. _____ beans
11. _____ cereal
12. _____ potato chips
13. _____ tea
14. _____ grapes
15. _____ apples

See the *Grammar Links* Website for more information about mobile home travel
in the United States.

9 | Numbers and Measure Words: Chain Game

Play the chain game as a class.

Student 1 says: "I went to the store, and I bought:
measure word/number + a noun beginning with the letter "A."

Student 2 repeats this and adds another *measure word or number + a noun*, this time beginning with the letter *B.* The game continues until someone makes a mistake or forgets.

Example: Student 1: I went to the store, and I bought a bag of apples.
          Student 2: I went to the store, and I bought a bag of apples and a box of bandages.
          Student 3: I went to the store, and I bought a bag of apples and a box of bandages
                     and two packages of cookies.

10 | Numbers and Measure Words: Your Own Creation

Imagine you are going to travel in a mobile home. Write a recipe to take with you on your trip. Be sure to give specific amounts (2 cups, 2½ teaspoons, etc.). Use some of the ingredients below or your own ingredients. Share your recipe with the class.

Ingredients

peanut butter	sugar	spaghetti	oranges	peas
bread	bananas	carrots	oil	vinegar
jelly	yogurt	raisins	rice	tortillas
salsa	cabbage	fish	ice cream	pudding
onions	lentils	ketchup	cookies	crackers
marshmallows	chocolate	maple syrup		

Note: Are any of the ingredients above new to you? Find them in your dictionary.

Example: Carmelita's Spaghetti and Peanut Butter
         1 cup of peanut butter   4 quarts of water
         1 pound of spaghetti   etc.

B. Discuss your recipes. Which ones sound good? Take a vote. Then try them!

11 | Numbers and Measure Words: Recipe from Home

A. Bring a real recipe from home to share with the class. Work with a partner. Tell your partner what you need for this recipe and see if she or he can tell it back to you. Correct any mistakes.

B. Work together as a class. Collect all of the recipes. Put them in a class cookbook. Try them!

Check your progress! Go to the Self-Test for Chapter 9 on the *Grammar Links* Website.

Pronouns and Possessives

Introductory Task: Great Adventure

Photo Safari Adventure

A. Listen to Lizzy talk about a photo. Circle the words you hear.

Hi. My name's Lizzy. I like adventure travel. Here, let (me / my) show you a picture.
₁
Then you'll know what I mean. In the front of the picture are (me / my) friends Frank and
₂
Blake. We all went on a photo safari together in Africa. (We / They) shot lots of photos of
₃
wild animals there. Oh, and that's our guide behind that tree.

He looks a little worried. I'm not sure why. There's (something / nothing) in
₄
the bushes in the background. It's difficult to see. . . . This isn't a very clear picture.
I took (its / it) with Frank's camera. (His / He) doesn't work as well as (mine / my).
₅ ₆ ₇
Anyway, Frank and Blake are a lot of fun. (Everybody / Nobody) really enjoys them. In this
₈
picture, Frank's getting (himself / him) a sandwich from his knapsack. Blake is standing
₉
next to (himself / him).
₁₀

---

adventure = excitement and/or danger. *photo safari* = a trip to take pictures of animals,
especially in Africa. *wild* = living in nature. *guide* = leader; someone who shows the way.

B. Look again at the picture on page 171. Work in small groups. Discuss:

1. Why do you think the guide is standing behind a tree? Why is he worried? What does he see in the bushes? Do Frank and Blake see the same thing?

2. Do you enjoy adventure travel? Are you an adventure traveler? Why or why not?

Pronouns and Possessive Adjectives I

FORM

PERSONAL PRONOUNS

SUBJECT PRONOUNS (S)*	OBJECT PRONOUNS (O)*
I	me
you	you
he	him
she	her
it	it
we	us
they	them

POSSESSIVES

POSSESSIVE ADJECTIVES (POSS. ADJ.)	POSSESSIVE PRONOUNS (POSS. PRO.)
my	mine
your	yours
his	his
her	hers
its	—
our	ours
their	theirs

REFLEXIVE PRONOUNS

myself
yourself
himself
herself
itself
ourselves
themselves

*See Appendix 12 for more information about subjects and objects.

Pronouns replace nouns. They include personal, reflexive, and possessive pronouns. Possessive adjectives come before nouns.

        poss.
s   adj.
I like **my** cat.

  s   reflexive
You hurt **yourself**.

poss.
 adj.   o
His mother loves **him**.

            poss.
            pro.
Which book is **ours**?

Pronouns and Possessive Adjectives I

1 **Identification of Pronouns and Possessive Adjectives:** Adventure Travel

Above each **boldfaced** word, write **S** (subject pronoun), **O** (object pronoun), **PA** (possessive adjective), **PP** (possessive pronoun), or **R** (reflexive pronoun).

  Adventure travel is becoming quite popular. **It** [S] is a very interesting kind of travel. Adventure travelers are not just looking for beautiful places to see. **They** are looking for adventure.

  Some people think adventure travel is new. But **it** is very old. In the thirteenth century, Marco Polo traveled thousands of miles, from Europe to China and other countries in Asia. Sometimes **he** traveled by **himself**. Sometimes **his** uncles traveled with **him**. **They** loved traveling for adventure.

  Once **you** begin adventure travel, **you** cannot stop. Excitement and freedom are **yours**, and **you** want more and more adventure. As soon as one adventure vacation ends, **you** find **yourself** planning **your** next adventure vacation. **We** owe a lot to the adventure travelers of the past and of the present. **They** help **us** push **ourselves** forward. **They** make **us** use **our** imaginations. **They** take **us** into the future.

 See the *Grammar Links* Website for more information about adventure vacations.

Pronouns and Possessive Adjectives II

FORM and FUNCTION

A. Personal Pronouns

1. Subject pronouns replace noun subjects.

    subject
    Greg and Blake are my friends. → **They** are my friends.

2. Object pronouns replace noun objects. They come after verbs and prepositions.

    direct object | indirect object
    I like **Greg and Blake**. They lent **Sheila** a canoe. → I like **them**. They lent **her** a canoe.

    object of a preposition
    They took a picture of **Kathy and me**. → They took a picture of **us**.

(continued on next page)

B. Possessive Adjectives and Pronouns

1. Possessive adjectives modify nouns and show possession.

   This is **my** camera. (This camera belongs to me; I own it.)

2. Possessive pronouns replace:

   • Possessive adjective + noun.

   Your camera is good; **her camera** is better.
   → Your camera is good; **hers** is better.

   • Possessive noun + noun.

   I lost my camera. I borrowed **John's camera**.
   → I lost my camera, I borrowed **his**.

3. Use *whose* to ask questions about possessions.

   Q: **Whose** airplane ticket is this?
   A: Mine. OR It's mine.

   Q: **Whose** is this?
   A: Mine. OR It's mine.

   Q: **Whose** shoes are in the hallway?
   A: They're Jane's shoes.

   Q: **Whose** are these?
   A: They're hers.

C. Reflexive Pronouns

1. Use a reflexive pronoun when the subject and the object in a sentence are the same.

   subject direct object
   Angela saw **Angela** in the water. → **Angela** saw **herself** in the water.

   subject object of preposition
   Angela likes to talk about **Angela**. → **Angela** likes to talk about **herself**.

   subject indirect object
   Angela bought **Angela** a new bike. → **Angela** bought **herself** a new bike.

2. Also use a reflexive after *by* to mean "alone."

   He climbed the mountain alone. = He climbed the mountain **by himself**.

1. To form possessive nouns:

    - Add an apostrophe (') to plural nouns that end in -s.

      the **babies'** books

    - Add ' or 's to singular nouns that end in -s.

      Charles' book OR **Charles's** book

    - Add 's to all other nouns.

      the **baby's** book

      the **children's** book

    - With two or more nouns together, add 's or ' only to the second noun.

      John and Mary's children

      the girls and the boys' teacher

2. Possessive adjectives and pronouns keep the same form before both singular and plural nouns. They do not have special singular or plural forms.

    This is **their camera**.

    These are not **their cameras**.
      NOT: These are ~~theirs~~ cameras.

We often use object pronouns after the verb *be*. In very formal writing, we use subject pronouns.

	MOST WRITING AND SPEAKING	VERY FORMAL WRITING
	Peter's in the photo. That's **him** in the back.	Peter is in the photograph. That is **he** in the back.

GRAMMAR PRACTICE 2

Pronouns and Possessive Adjectives II

2 **Pronouns and Possessive Adjectives:** Journey to the Center of the Earth

Complete the story with the correct words from the boxes. Use each word only once.

they	them	their	✓theirs	themselves

Clara and Martin love adventure vacations. Many people take interesting vacations, but

theirs _____ are especially exciting. Clara and Martin take all of their adventure
          1

vacations on _____ bicycles. They enjoy _____ very
              2   3

much on these trips. _____ are planning their next trip now. It will take
                      4

_____ from Cairo, Egypt, across the desert to the Dead Sea.
5

it	it	its	itself

The Dead Sea is an interesting place. _____ 6 _____ is
the lowest spot on the earth, 1,300 feet below "sea level," the usual
level of the sea. The rocks and sand on _____ 7 _____
shores are pure white. They are covered with salt crystals. In fact,
the Dead Sea "cleans" _____ 8 _____ with salt. It contains almost
ten times more salt than any other body of water on the earth. Not much grows
in _____ 9 _____, so it is very clear and clean.

she	her	her	hers	herself

The trip from Cairo to the Dead Sea will take about
one month. Clara and Martin will ride almost
1,000 miles through the desert in very hot (often
over 100 degrees Fahrenheit) weather. Before she
goes, Clara needs to buy _____ 10 _____
a new bike. _____ 11 _____ won't work
on sand. Clara will take _____ 12 _____
old bike to a bike shop. They will give _____ 13 _____ some money
for it. _____ 14 _____ will use that money to buy a new bike.

Dead Sea

he	him	his	his	himself

Last year Martin cycled by _____ 15 _____ in the desert in Arizona. He had no
trouble with _____ 16 _____ bike, so _____ 17 _____ doesn't need a
new bike for this trip. _____ 18 _____ is ready. It will probably take
_____ 19 _____ across the desert with no problems.

| you | you | your | yours | yourself |

Why do Martin and Clara want to go to the Dead Sea on bicycles? Does this sound like

a crazy idea to _____ ? Martin talks about his feelings: "Imagine
                        20

_____ gliding down, down, down off a high hill to the very lowest
        21

spot—the center of the earth. That is a thrilling experience! Then

_____ see this calm shining body of water, with ghostly white shores
        22

all around it. You stick _____ toe in, then your whole body. Your wait
                                23

is over! You finally succeed after 1,000 miles of heat and sand and sun. You drift and float

above the center of the earth. Victory is _____ !"
                                                  24

| we | us | our | ours | ourselves |

Clara says: "Martin and I have different reasons for our adventure travels, it's true.

But that doesn't matter. Traveling on _____ bikes makes
                                              25

_____ both happy. _____ enjoy
        26   27

_____ . _____ is a good life."
        28   29

3 Pronouns and Possessive Adjectives: King of the Mountain!

Rod is telling his friend Jeff about his adventure vacation to Mount Kilimanjaro in Africa. Listen to their conversation. Write the words you hear.

Rod: Well, here is a photo of Mount Kilimanjaro. __It__ 1 _____ is the highest mountain

in Africa. _____ 2 spent five days climbing to the top and back down.

Jeff: Wow! _____ 3 really beautiful! And what a great photo! _____ 4

camera did you use?

Rod: Well, _____ 5 doesn't take very good photos, but _____ 6

friend Fred came with _____ 7 on the trip. I used _____ 8 .

Here's a picture of Fred. That's _____ 9 on the left.

Jeff: And _____ 10 big backpack is that in the photo?

Rod: Fred's. He carried it all the way to the top by _____ 11 ! It was heavy!

Jeff: And _____ 12 are the other people in the picture?

Rod: We were traveling with three other climbers. _____ 13 were from England.

That's _____ 14 on the right.

Jeff: You must be pretty proud of _____ 15 . I tried mountain climbing

_____ 16 once, but I didn't like it very much. I prefer sea level.

4 **Nouns to Pronouns:** An Impossible World!

Change the **boldfaced** nouns to pronouns and possessive adjectives.
Make all the other necessary changes.

1. Larry and Charles are talking.

   Larry: Hi, Charles! How was ~~Charles'~~ [your] vacation?

   Charles: Oh, hi, Larry. ~~Charles'~~ [My] vacation was fine. ~~Charles~~ [I] took ~~Charles'~~ [my] family on an adventure vacation. ~~Charles and Charles' family~~ [We] had a great time!

2. Grace and Alena are talking.

   Grace: Say, Alena, did Lizzy and Kathy give **Alena** back **Alena's** map?

   Alena: No, Grace, **Lizzy and Kathy** didn't. **Lizzy and Kathy** gave **Alena's** map to **Grace**. Where is **the map**?

   Grace: Where is what? What are **Grace and Alena** talking about? **Grace is** confused!

3. Rose and Kyle are talking.

   Rose: Jane lost **Jane's** camera on **Jane, Kyle, Rose, Andrea, Peter and Donald's** adventure trip last week. **Does Kyle** know where the camera is?

   Kyle: **Kyle** found **Jane's** camera in **Kyle's** backpack. **Kyle** put **the camera** there by mistake. **Kyle** will bring **the camera** to **Rose** today.

   Rose: Oh, no! Not to **Rose**! Could **Kyle** please take **the camera** to Donald and Peter's house? Jane wants to give **the camera** to **Donald and Peter**. **Donald and Peter** need **the camera** this week. Jane bought **Jane** a new camera. **Jane** doesn't need **Jane's** old camera anymore.

Correct the errors in the story. There are eight errors with pronouns and possessive adjectives. The first error is corrected for you.

Last year my family and I took a wonderful adventure vacation. We gave ~~us~~ *ourselves* a trip to the Canadian Arctic. We traveled across the Ungava Peninsula in dogsleds. We stayed with Inuit families along the way. We slept in they houses, and we ate ours meals with them. Theirs hospitality was wonderful. They served us hot meals—caribou stew and whale blubber. I didn't think I was going to like whale blubber, but its was very tasty!

Caribou

Everyone in my family learned a lot on this vacation. My parents were quite proud of theirselves and their success. My brother learned a lot, too. He enjoyed hisself very much, but he prefers warm weather. As for me, I had a wonderful time. I am still dreaming about her adventure in the cold, white north.

> *whale blubber* = fat from whales, used as food by the Inuit.

6 **Pronouns and Possessive Adjectives:** Create an Adventure

A. Choose a method of transportation from Column A and a person or people from Column B. Use them to create an adventure vacation. Write at least five sentences. Use at least one personal pronoun, one possessive pronoun, one possessive adjective, and one reflexive pronoun in your description.

Column A

a canoe

a balloon

feet

a submarine

a four-wheel drive truck

a snowmobile

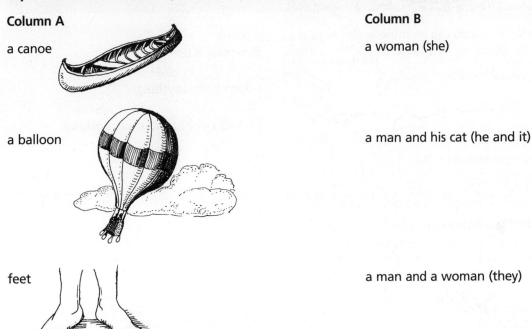

Column B

a woman (she)

a man and his cat (he and it)

a man and a woman (they)

you and two other people (we)

you alone (I)

the person you are talking to (you)

Example: A man and his cat are going on a balloon adventure. The man is happy, and he is preparing for his trip. . . .

See the *Grammar Links* Website for a complete model paragraph for this assignment.

B. Share your description with the rest of the class. Discuss the different vacations. Which ones are the most adventurous? Which one(s) would you most enjoy? Why?

Indefinite Pronouns

FORM and FUNCTION

A. Overview

Indefinite pronouns can be subjects and objects. They can also come after the verb *be*.

subject
Everyone is here now.

object
I don't want **anything**.

after *be*
I heard a noise, but it was **nothing**.

Indefinite pronouns include:

SOME	ANY	NO	EVERY
someone	anyone	no one	everyone
somebody	anybody	nobody	everybody
something	anything	nothing	everything

B. Indefinite Pronouns for People and Things

1. The endings *-one* and *-body* refer to people.

   Someone/Somebody took my camera. (Some person took my camera.)

2. The ending *-thing* refers to things.

   I want **something** for dessert. (I want some kind of dessert.)

3. Indefinite pronouns that begin with *no-* mean "not one person" or "not one thing."

   There was **nobody** in the room. (There was not one person in the room.)

   There was **nothing** on the plate. (There was not one thing on the plate.)

   Don't use *not* and an indefinite pronoun with *no-* in the same sentence.

   I saw **no one**.
   NOT: I ~~didn't see~~ no one.

4. We use indefinite pronouns with *some-* in affirmative sentences. *Any-* replaces *some-* in most negative statements and questions.

   Affirmative: I have **something** for you.

   Negative: I don't have **anything** for you.

   Question: Is there **anything** in this bag?

C. Verb Agreement with Indefinite Pronouns

Indefinite pronoun subjects take singular verbs, even when their meaning is plural.

Everybody **is** here.
NOT: Everybody ~~are~~ here.

	FORMAL WRITING	SPEAKING AND INFORMAL WRITING
1. Indefinite pronouns are singular. However, we often use the plural pronouns *they*, *them*, and *their* with these words in everyday speaking and writing. In very formal writing, we use singular pronouns.	Someone left **his or her** jacket in the restaurant.	Someone left **their** jacket in the restaurant.
	He or she can pick it up at the counter.	**They** can pick it up at the counter.
	Please tell **him or her** to come and get it.	Please tell **them** to come and get it.
2. We often use contractions of indefinite pronouns with *is* in speaking and informal writing.	**Everyone is** here.	**Everyone's** here.

Indefinite Pronouns

7 **Indefinite Pronouns:** Present and Accounted For!

Read the conversation among hikers returning from a long hike. Circle the correct indefinite pronouns.

Julia: Let's see. Is everybody here? I see only five people. (Somebody's / Something's)
1
missing! Who is it? Oh, yes. It's Fred! Where's Fred? Does (anyone / anything) know?
2
Oh, there he is, behind that tree. Okay. Now, does (everybody / everything) have all
3
their belongings?

Rod: I don't have my passport. I asked (everyone / no one), but (nobody / anybody)
4 5
knows where it is! Maybe (someone / anyone) took it!
6

Julia: Let's look around here for it. What's that over there?

Rod: Over where? I don't see (anything / nothing).
7

Julia: Over there on the ground.

Rod: Oh, that's just someone's / no one's) boot. Whose boot is that?
8

Patty: Boot? Oh, thank you for finding it. It's mine. I was looking for it. I want to put it
back on. . . . Wait a minute. There's (something / nothing) inside my boot. . . .
9
Whose passport is this? (Somebody / Something) put their passport in my boot!
10

8 Indefinite Pronouns: Find Someone Who . . .

A. Work with a partner. Take turns interviewing each other. Check the things that are true.

Use questions like: *Do you enjoy . . . ? Do you know what . . . is? Do you want to . . . ?*

My partner:

_____ enjoys trekking   _____ knows what skydiving is

_____ likes camping in the desert   _____ knows how to fly an airplane

_____ enjoys scuba diving   _____ knows what spelunking is

_____ wants to go on a safari   _____ enjoys rock climbing

_____ wants to go to the Arctic Circle   _____ likes camping in the jungle

> *trekking* = making a long trip on foot. *jungle* = tropical forest, such as the forest in the Amazon. *scuba diving* = swimming in deep water with air tanks for breathing.

B. What are the results of the interview? Which of the activities in Part A do students in the class enjoy? One student asks the class questions to find out. Use *anybody* or *anyone* in the questions. Count the number of students for each answer. Write the number on the board.

Example: *Does anyone enjoy trekking?*

Are there questions **everybody** answered "yes"? What are they?

Are there questions **nobody** answered "yes"? What are they?

Discuss: Were you surprised by any of your classmates' answers? If yes, which ones?

9 Indefinite Pronouns: Quick Quiz

Write **C** next to each correct sentence and **I** next to each incorrect sentence. Then rewrite the incorrect sentences, correcting the errors. (Sometimes there is more than one possible way to correct a sentence.

1. ___C___   Did anyone see Fred? _____

   _____

2. ___I___   Are everybody happy?   *Is everybody happy?* _____

   _____

3. _____   Nobody didn't lose their boots. _____

   _____

4. _____ Everybody climbed that mountain. _____

_____

5. _____ Does everyone have their cameras? _____

_____

6. _____ Julia didn't see no one on the trail. _____

_____

7. _____ Someone forgot their backpack. _____

_____

8. _____ Everyone enjoy adventure vacations. _____

_____

9. _____ Someone left their camera here. They will need it. _____

_____

10. _____ We don't have anything to do tonight. Let's plan our next adventure vacation!

_____

 Check your progress! Go to the Self-Test for
Chapter 10 on the *Grammar Links* Website.

Wrap-up Activities

1 Travel in the North: EDITING

Correct the errors in this article. There are 15 errors with nouns, pronouns, possessive adjectives, articles, quantifiers, and numbers. (Sometimes there is more than one possible correction.) The first error is corrected for you.

T his vehicle travels up to 70 miles a̶ hour. *(an)* It travels on the ground, but it doesn't have wheels. And it doesn't have a engine! What is it? It's sled.

People used sleds in ancient times. A first sleds were animal skins. Travelers pulled these sleds behind them. But animal skin sleds were slow. Their didn't slide smoothly. So ancient travelers added runners to they. These runners were long pieces of bone or wood. Travelers put the runners under the animal skins. The runners made their sleds travel faster and more smoothly, but pulling a sled still took several energy. No one didn't like this very much. So people began training animals to pull their sleds. Then sleds became very fast.

Each years in northern countries, many people gather together for special dogsled races. One famous race, the Iditarod, takes place in the early Spring in northern alaska. In this race, teams of dogs and humans travel from Anchorage to Nome— over 1,000 miles of difficult land. There are much challenges: deep snow, unpredictable weather, and wild animals. Dogs often wear boots to protect theirselves from ice. Approximately 75 team compete each year. Some teams don't finish the long trek. But everybody have a great adventure!

 See the *Grammar Links* Website for more information about the Iditarod dogsled race.

Imagine you are going "camping" at the bottom of the sea! You will live in a "sea bubble" for three days. The bubble has lots of glass on the outside, so you can see all of the interesting fish and plants living in the sea.

Step 1 Read the information in this brochure about your adventure.

FACT SHEET

In your bubble you will have:

* Oxygen—for only three days

* Water—for showers but no clean drinking water

* Sleeping compartment with a shower

* A small bed—no blankets

* A small cooking stove and refigerator—no food

Other information about your bubble:

Heat: Heat from the sun during the day. No heat at night.

Night temperature inside the bubble: 32° Fahrenheit (0°Celsius)

Electricity: turned off at 10:00 every night

Equipment needed to leave bubble and explore: pressurized diving suit, extra oxygen, head lamp

You must take everything you need for three days.

You may take no more than 40 pounds of personal belongings with you in the bubble.

Step 2 Look at the list below. As a group, decide what one person will need for three days. Give exact amounts, and add up the weight. Remember! Don't pack more than 40 pounds. (Note: 16 ounces = 1 pound.)

beans (1 can = 1 pound)
rice (1 bag = 1 pound)
apples (1 apple = 4 ounces)
cereal (1 box = 1 pound)
milk (1 quart = 1 pound)
coffee (1 can = 1 pound)
drinking water (1 gallon = 8 pounds)
pressurized diving suit (10 pounds)
towel (1 pound)
soap (1 bar = 4 ounces)
warm coat (5 pounds)
1 camera (1 pound)
film for the camera (4 ounces)

book to read (8 ounces)
journal to write in (8 ounces)
headlamp (1 pound)
toothpaste (1 tube = 4 ounces)
toothbrush (4 ounces)
shampoo (1 bottle = 8 ounces)
extra oxygen (10 pounds)
battery-operated reading light (1 pound)
1 warm sleeping bag (5 pounds)
clean clothes (5 pounds)
battery-operated heater (10 pounds)
batteries for the heater (8 ounces)

Step 3 Present your list to the rest of the class. Discuss: Did everyone agree on the most important items?

3 A Place I Love: WRITING/SPEAKING

Step 1 Bring to class a picture of a city or country place you love to visit. Write at least five sentences about this place. Concentrate on using articles, quantifiers, and pronouns in your description.

Example: Here is a picture of a place I love to visit. It is a small town in the
Rocky Mountains. The people there are very friendly. . . .

 See the *Grammar Links* Website for a complete model paragraph for this activity.

Step 2 Read your description to your classmates. Show them your photo. Compare and discuss places.

4 Whose Is What? SPEAKING/LISTENING

Step 1 Bring to class an object that you like very much and that someone gave you. DON'T LET THE CLASS SEE IT AHEAD OF TIME!

Step 2 Student 1: Put all the objects in a bag.
Student 2: Pick out an object and ask: "Whose _____

is this?" or "Whose _____ are these?"
Whole class: Guess who the owner is.

Step 3 When the class guesses your object, say, "Yes, it's mine." Then explain why you like your object. Describe the person who gave it to you. Use pronouns and quantifiers in your description. Try to talk for 30 seconds without stopping!

Example: This watch is mine. I like it a lot. It always keeps good time. I also like its
color and shape. My aunt Flora gave it to me. Everybody loves my aunt Flora.
She is my mother's sister. She lives in Montana with the rest of my family.

Simple Present Tense of the Verb *Be*

FORM

A. Affirmative Statements

SUBJECT	*BE*	
I	**am**	tall.
You		
We	**are**	tall.
They		
He		
She	**is**	tall.
It		

B. Negative Statements

SUBJECT	*BE + NOT*	
I	**am not**	tall.
	'm not	
You	**are not**	
We	**aren't**	tall.
They	**'re not**	
He	**is not**	
She	**isn't**	tall.
It	**'s not**	

C. *Yes/No* Questions and Short Answers

QUESTIONS

BE	SUBJECT	
Am	I	tall?
Are	you	
	we	tall?
	they	
Is	he	
	she	tall?
	it	

SHORT ANSWERS

YES			NO		
Yes,	I	**am.**	No,	I	**am not.**
					'm not.
Yes,	you		No,	you	**are not.**
	we	**are.**		we	**aren't.**
	they			they	**'re not.**
Yes,	he		No,	he	**is not.**
	she	**is.**		she	**isn't.**
	it			it	**'s not.**

D. *Wh-* Questions and Answers

QUESTIONS

WH- WORD	*BE*	SUBJECT
Where	**am**	I?
Who	**are**	you?
		we?
		they?
Where	**is**	he?
		she?
		it?

ANSWERS

ANSWERS
In the hospital.
Doctors.
In the hospital.

Pronunciation Rules for the Third Person Singular Form of the Simple Present Tense

The -*s* ending is pronounced three different ways:

- /s/ after the voiceless sounds /p/, /t/, /k/, and /f/.

- /z/ after the voiced sounds /b/, /d/, /g/, /v/, /th/, /m/, /n/, /ng/, /l/, /r/, and all vowel sounds.

- /iz/ after the sounds /s/, /z/, /sh/, /zh/, /ch/, /j/, and /ks/.

stops	gets	takes	laughs

robs	gives	remains	hears
adds	bathes	sings	agrees
begs	seems	tells	knows

passes	catches
freezes	judges (ge = /j/)
rushes	relaxes (x = /ks/)
massages (ge = /zh/)	

Spelling Rules for -*ing* Verb Forms

1. Most verbs: Base form of verb + -*ing*

   walk → walk**ing**   order → order**ing**

2. Verbs that end in -*e*: Drop -*e*. Add -*ing*.

   write → writ**ing**   decide → decid**ing**

3. Verbs that end in -*ie*: Change -*ie* to -*y*. Add -*ing*.

   tie → **tying**   lie → **lying**

4. Verbs that end in consonant + vowel + consonant: Double the final consonant. Add -*ing*.

   run → ru**nning**   permit → permi**tting**

   BUT: Do not double the final consonant when:

   - The last syllable is not stressed.
   - The last consonant is *w*, *x*, or *y*.

   lísten → listen**ing**

   allow → allow**ing**   box → box**ing**

   play → play**ing**

Spelling Rules for the Simple Past Tense of Regular Verbs

1. Most verbs: Add -ed.

   walk → walk**ed**   order → order**ed**

2. Verbs that end in -e: Add -d.

   live → live**d**   decide → decide**d**

3. Verbs that end in a consonant + y: Change -y to -i. Add -ed.

   bury → bur**ied**

4. Verbs that end in consonant + vowel + consonant: Double the final consonant. Add -ed.

   shop → shop**ped**   permit → permit**ted**

   BUT: Do not double the final consonant when:

   - The last syllable is not stressed.

     lísten → listen**ing**

   - The last consonant is w, x, or y.

     allow → allo**wing**   box → bo**xing**

     play → pla**ying**

Pronunciation Rules for the Simple Past Tense of Regular Verbs

The -d ending is pronounced three different ways:

- /t/ after the voiceless sounds /f/, /k/, /p/, /s/, /sh/, /ch/, and /ks/.

laughed	clapped	wished	waxed
talked	passed	watched	

- /d/ after the voiced sounds /b/, /g/, /j/, /m/, /n/, /ng/, /l/, /r/, /th/, /v/, /z/, /zh/, and all vowel sounds.

robbed	bathed
begged	waved
judged (ge = /j/)	surprised
seemed	massaged (ge = /zh/)
remained	played
banged	enjoyed
called	cried
ordered	

- /ɪd/ after the sounds /t/ and /d/.

started	needed

Irregular Verbs

BASE FORM	PAST	PAST PARTICIPLE	BASE FORM	PAST	PAST PARTICIPLE
be	was, were	been	forget	forgot	forgotten
beat	beat	beaten	forgive	forgave	forgiven
become	became	become	freeze	froze	frozen
begin	began	begun	get	got	gotten
bend	bent	bent	give	gave	given
bite	bit	bitten	go	went	gone
bleed	bled	bled	grow	grew	grown
blow	blew	blown	have	had	had
break	broke	broken	hear	heard	heard
bring	brought	brought	hide	hid	hidden
build	built	built	hit	hit	hit
burn	burned/burnt	burned/burnt	hold	held	held
buy	bought	bought	hurt	hurt	hurt
catch	caught	caught	keep	kept	kept
choose	chose	chosen	know	knew	known
come	came	come	lay	laid	laid
cost	cost	cost	lead	led	led
cut	cut	cut	leap	leaped/leapt	leaped/leapt
dig	dug	dug	leave	left	left
do	did	done	lend	lent	lent
draw	drew	drawn	let	let	let
dream	dreamed/dreamt	dreamed/dreamt	lie	lay	lain
drink	drank	drunk	light	lit/lighted	lit/lighted
drive	drove	driven	lose	lost	lost
eat	ate	eaten	make	made	made
fall	fell	fallen	mean	meant	meant
feed	fed	fed	meet	met	met
feel	felt	felt	mistake	mistook	mistaken
fight	fought	fought	pay	paid	paid
find	found	found	prove	proved	proved/proven
fly	flew	flown	put	put	put
forbid	forbade	forbidden	quit	quit	quit
forecast	forecast	forecast	read	read	read

Irregular Verbs

BASE FORM	PAST	PAST PARTICIPLE	BASE FORM	PAST	PAST PARTICIPLE
rid	rid	rid	spend	spent	spent
ride	rode	ridden	spread	spread	spread
ring	rang	rung	spring	sprang	sprung
rise	rose	risen	stand	stood	stood
run	ran	run	steal	stole	stolen
say	said	said	strike	struck	struck
see	saw	seen	swear	swore	sworn
seek	sought	sought	sweep	swept	swept
sell	sold	sold	swim	swam	swum
send	sent	sent	swing	swung	swung
set	set	set	take	took	taken
shake	shook	shaken	teach	taught	taught
shave	shaved	shaved/shaven	tear	tore	torn
shine	shined/shone	shined/shone	tell	told	told
shoot	shot	shot	think	thought	thought
show	showed	showed/shown	throw	threw	thrown
shut	shut	shut	understand	understood	understood
sing	sang	sung	upset	upset	upset
sink	sank	sunk	wake	woke	woken
sit	sat	sat	wear	wore	worn
sleep	slept	slept	wet	wet	wet
slide	slid	slid	win	won	won
speak	spoke	spoken	wind	wound	wound
speed	sped	sped	write	wrote	written

Simple Past Tense of *Be*

FORM

A. Affirmative Statements

SUBJECT	*BE*	
I		
He		
She	**was**	tall.
It		
You		
We	**were**	tall.
They		

B. Negative Statements

SUBJECT	*BE + NOT*	
I		
He	**was not**	
She	**wasn't**	tall.
It		
You		
We	**were not**	tall.
They	**weren't**	

C. *Yes/No* Questions and Short Answers

QUESTIONS

BE	SUBJECT	
	I	
Was	he	tall?
	she	
	it	
	you	
Were	we	tall?
	they	

SHORT ANSWERS

YES			
	I		
Yes,	he	**was.**	
	she		
	it		
Yes,	you		
	we	**were.**	
	they		

NO			
	I		
No,	he	**was not.**	
	she	**wasn't.**	
	it		
No,	you		
	we	**were not.**	
	they	**weren't.**	

D. *Wh-* Questions and Answers

QUESTIONS

WH- WORD	*BE*	SUBJECT
		I?
Where	**was**	he?
		she?
		it?
		you?
Who	**were**	we?
		they?

ANSWERS

In the hospital.

Doctors.

Spelling Rules for Regular Plural Count Nouns

- Most nouns: Add -s.

room → rooms	office → offices
day → days	studio → studios

- Nouns that end in -ch, -sh, -ss, -x, or -z: Add -es.

lunch → lunches	box → boxes
brush → brushes	quiz → quizzes
kiss → kisses	

- Nouns ending in a consonant + -y: Drop -y. Add -ies.

dormitory → dormitories	story → stories

- Nouns ending in -f or -fe: Drop -f or -fe. Add -ves.

shelf → shelves	knife → knives
Exceptions: belief → beliefs, chief → chiefs, roof → roofs	

- A few nouns ending in a consonant + -o: Add -es.

hero → heroes	potato → potatoes
mosquito → mosquitoes	tomato → tomatoes

Pronunciation Rules for Regular Plural Count Nouns

The -s ending is pronounced as:

- /s/ after the voiceless sounds /p/, /t/, /k/, /f/, and /th/.

cups	hats	books	cuffs	paths

- /z/ after the voiced sounds /b/, /d/, /g/, /v/, /th/, /m/, /n/, /ng/, /l/, /r/, and all vowel sounds.

jobs	knives	bones	bears
kids	lathes	things	days
legs	dreams	bells	potatoes

- /ɪz/ after the sounds /s/, /z/, /sh/, /zh/, /ch/, /j/, and /ks/.

classes	churches
breezes	judges (ge = /j/)
dishes	taxes (x = /ks/)
massages (ge = /zh/)	

Common Irregular Plural Nouns

SINGULAR	PLURAL	SINGULAR	PLURAL	SINGULAR	PLURAL	SINGULAR	PLURAL
child	children	goose	geese	person	people	woman	women
deer	deer	man	men	sheep	sheep		
fish	fish	mouse	mice	species	species		
foot	feet	ox	oxen	tooth	teeth		

Common Noncount Nouns

1. Names of groups of similar items:

baggage	equipment	furniture	jewelry	mail	stuff
cash	food	garbage	luggage	makeup	trash
clothing	fruit	homework	machinery	money	traffic

(**Note:** These groups often have individual parts that can be counted; for example, clothing is made up of different pieces—dresses, shirts, coats, etc.)

2. Liquids:

coffee	gasoline	juice	lotion	oil	sauce	soda	syrup	vinegar	wine
cream	honey	ketchup	milk	rubbing alcohol	shampoo	soup	tea	water	

3. Solids:

aspirin	cabbage	chocolate	garlic	ice cream	meat	seafood	wool
bacon	cake	cotton	glass	jam	paper	soap	yogurt
beef	candy	film	gold	Jell-O	pasta	spaghetti	
bread	cheese	fish	hair	jelly	pie	toothpaste	
butter	chicken (as food)	food	ice	lettuce	pizza	wood	

4. Particles:

cereal	corn	dust	grass	pepper	salt	spice	wheat
chalk	dirt	flour	hair	rice	sand	sugar	

5. Gases:

air	fog	hydrogen	smog	smoke	steam

(continued on next page)

Common Noncount Nouns (continued)

6. Natural phenomena:

cold	electricity	hail	light	mist	rain	snow	temperature	weather	
darkness	fire	heat	lightning	space	scenery	sunshine	warmth	wind	

7. Abstract ideas:

art	education	happiness	joy	luck	quiet	trouble
beauty	entertainment	health	knowledge	music	space	truth
comfort	freedom	homework	laughter	news*	time	wealth
competition	friendship	honesty	life	noise	traffic	weightlessness
courage	fun	information	love	peace	travel	work

8. Fields of study:

accounting	biology	economics	geometry	literature	physics*	speech
art	business	engineering	journalism	mathematics*	science	writing
astronomy	chemistry	geography	linguistics	music	sociology	

*Some noncount nouns, such as *news*, *mathematics*, and *physics*, end in -*s*. These nouns look plural, but they are not; they always take a singular verb.

Noun Functions

In an English sentence, a noun can be:

- the **subject** of the sentence.

  Henry Ford invented the automobile.

- the **subject complement** (for example, after *be* or *become*), when it renames or identifies the subject.

  Henry Ford was an **inventor**.

- the **direct object**, when it directly receives the action of the verb.

  Henry Ford invented the **automobile**.

- the **indirect object**, when it indirectly receives the action.

  Henry Ford gave his **wife** an automobile. (In this sentence, *automobile* is the direct object. Ford gave an automobile. *Wife* is the indirect object.)

- the **object of a preposition**. Prepositions include words such as *through*, *in*, *of*, *to*, and *on*.

  Henry's wife drove her automobile to the **beach**.

Spelling Rules and Irregular Forms for Adverbs of Manner

- Many adverbs of manner are formed from adjective + -ly.

sad → sad**ly**	beautiful → beautiful**ly**
slow → slow**ly**	

- Adjectives that end in -y: Drop the -y and add -ily.

eas~~y~~ → eas**ily**	happ~~y~~ → happ**ily**

- Adjectives that end in -ic or -ical: Add -ally.

tragic → tragic**ally**	physical → physic**ally**

- Irregular forms (adjective and adverb forms are the same):

fast	hard	right	wrong	loud
long	friendly	lively	lonely	lovely

- The adverbial form of the adjective *good* is *well*.

Common Adjective + Preposition Combinations

afraid of	crazy about	famous for	full of	jealous of	responsible for	safe from	sorry for
bad for	familiar with	fond of	good for	proud of	sad about	similar to	sure about

Common Phrasal Verbs and Their Meanings

Phrasal Verbs Without Objects

catch up	reach the same place	show up	appear
drop out	leave an activity or group	slow down	become slower
grow up	become adult	take off	start (to fly or move)
run out	come to the end	turn up	come; visit unexpectedly
settle down	become comfortable	work out	exercise

Phrasal Verbs With Objects

bring up	educate (a child)	let down	disappoint; not keep a promise
build up	make stronger	look up	find written facts about
call off	cancel (a plan)	make up	1. invent 2. replace; compensate
check out	find information about		
figure out	discover (an answer)	pick up	get; collect
give up	stop doing (an activity)	point out	tell
keep up	continue		

(continued on next page)

Common Phrasal Verbs and Their Meanings (continued)

Phrasal Verbs With Objects

show off	want people to see	turn down	1. make quieter 2. say no to (an invitation)
sign up	register; add (a name) to a list	turn off	stop from working
take off	make (time) free	turn up	make louder
try out	test	work out	solve (a problem)

APPENDIX 16

Common Verb + Preposition Combinations

believe in	come from	happen to	live on	pay for	think of
belong to	concentrate on	hear about	look after	recover from	wait for
care about	depend on	know about	look at	talk to	worry about
care for	forget about	listen to	look for	think about	

APPENDIX 17

Common Three-Word Verbs and Their Meanings

come up with	discover (an idea)	get down to	begin (work)
cut down on	use or have less	get through with	finish
drop in on	visit unexpectedly	keep up with	go at the same speed as
face up to	confront; meet bravely	meet up with	meet unexpectedly
get along with	enjoy their company	put up with	tolerate

APPENDIX 18

Adjectives ending in -ing and -ed; -ed Adjective + Preposition Combinations

PRESENT PARTICIPLES (-ING FORMS)	PAST PARTICIPLES + PREPOSITIONS (-ED FORMS)	PRESENT PARTICIPLES (-ING FORMS)	PAST PARTICIPLES + PREPOSITIONS (-ED FORMS)
amazing	amazed at	depressing	depressed about/by
amusing	amused by	disappointing	disappointed with/in
annoying	annoyed by/with	disgusting	disgusted with
boring	bored with	exciting	excited about
confusing	confused by	exhausting	exhausted from

(continued on next page)

Adjectives ending in -ing and -ed; -ed Adjective + Preposition Combinations (continued)

PRESENT PARTICIPLES (-ING FORMS)	PAST PARTICIPLES + PREPOSITIONS (-ED FORMS)	PRESENT PARTICIPLES (-ING FORMS)	PAST PARTICIPLES + PREPOSITIONS (-ED FORMS)
fascinating	fascinated by	satisfying	satisfied with
frightening	frightened of	shocking	shocked by
inspiring	inspired by	terrifying	terrified of
interesting	interested in	tiring	tired of
pleasing	pleased with	worrying	worried about

APPENDIX 19

Comparative and Superlative Adjectives and Adverbs

ADJECTIVES AND ADVERBS	SIMPLE FORM	COMPARATIVE FORM	SUPERLATIVE FORM	WHAT DO I USE? -ER/-EST OR MORE/MOST?
One-syllable adjectives and adverbs	clean	cleaner	cleanest	Use -er and -est.
	fast	faster	fastest	
	slow	slower*	slowest*	
	big	bigger*	biggest*	
Most two-syllable adjectives and adverbs	active	more active	most active	Use more and most.
	frequent	more frequent	most frequent	
	frequently	more frequently	most frequently	
	quickly	more quickly	most quickly	
Two-syllable adjectives ending in -y, -ow, -er, -some or -ite	lonely	lonelier**	loneliest	Use -er or -est. OR Use more and most.
		more lonely	most lonely	
	narrow	narrower	narrowest	
		more narrow	most narrow	
All adjectives and adverbs of three or more syllables	beautiful	more beautiful	most beautiful	Use more and most.
	spontaneously	more spontaneously	most spontaneously	

*For one-syllable adjectives or adverbs that end with a single vowel + a consonant, double the final consonant before adding -er or -est. Do not double the final consonants x, w, and y.

**For two syllable adjectives ending in a consonant + -y, change the -y to -i and add -er or -est.

Verbs Commonly Followed by Gerunds

admit	consider	endure	finish	involve	miss	recommend	suggest
anticipate	delay	enjoy	forgive	justify	practice	report	support
appreciate	discuss	escape	go	keep (continue)	prevent	resist	tolerate
avoid	dislike	explain	imagine	mention	quit	risk	understand

Verbs Commonly Followed by Infinitives

advise	attempt	demand	hesitate	manage	pretend	struggle
agree	claim	deserve	hope	need	promise	tend
appear	consent	expect	intend	offer	refuse	wait
arrange	decide	fail	learn	plan	seem	want

Grammar Glossary

adjective   A word that modifies a noun. Adjectives often come before the nouns they modify. They also come after linking verbs.

>A **beautiful** cat walked in the door.
>The cows looked **wild**.

adverb   A word that modifies a verb, an adjective, another adverb, or a complete sentence.

>He ran **quickly**.
>Beans are **very** healthy.
>He ran **really** quickly.
>**Yesterday**, I went fishing.

affirmative statement   A positive sentence. Affirmative statements do not usually include *not*.

>I **like** chocolate.

articles   The words *a/an* and *the*. Articles introduce and identify nouns.

>**a** dog   **an** apple
>**the** cat   **the** apples

as . . . as   Used with adjectives, adverbs, nouns, and verbs to talk about two things that are equal or very similar.

>Europe is **as rainy as** North America.
>Boston has **as much snow as** Minneapolis.

auxiliary verb (also called *helping verb*) A verb that is used with a main verb to make questions and negative sentences and to help make tenses. *Do, have*, and *be* are often used as auxiliary verbs. The modals (*e.g., can, should, will*) are also auxiliary verbs.

>Rachel **does**n't have time for lunch.
>Peter **has** arrived.
>**Is** she reading?
>They **can** come with us.

base form of a verb   A verb without *to* in front of it or any endings after it; an infinitive without *to*.

>**make   do   eat   be**

clause   A group of related words that has a subject and a verb.

>**If I call you . . .**
>**Today is Sunday.**
>**. . . when he comes.**

common noun   A noun that is not the name of a particular person, place, thing, or idea.

>**dog   sugar   people**
>**houses   honesty**

comparative   Form of an adjective, adverb, noun, or verb used to describe two things that are different.

>The earth is **bigger than** the moon.
>Jack exercises **more than** Joe does.

conditional sentence   A sentence that contains an *if* clause and a main clause. The *if* clause states the condition. The main clause states the expected or imagined result.

>**If you heat water, it boils.**
>**If you go, I will go, too.**

contraction   The combination of two words into one. In contractions, letters are replaced with an apostrophe (').

>They will → **They'll**   We are → **We're**

count noun   A noun that names a person, place, thing, or idea that can be counted. There can be one, two, three, or more.

>**a boy   2 boys   3 boys**

definite article   The word *the. The* is used with singular, plural, and noncount nouns when both the speaker and the listener are thinking about the same noun.

>**The sun** is shining brightly today.

direct object   A noun, pronoun, or noun phrase that directly receives the action of the verb in a sentence.

>Jack ate **the cake**.   Ramon likes **me**.

general quantifier   A quantifier that describes a general amount or quantity.

> **several** people   **a lot of** sugar
> **a few** days

gerund   The *-ing* form of a verb, used as a noun.

> I enjoy **working**.
> We go **fishing** every summer.

imperative   A type of sentence used for making offers and requests and for giving orders. The verb in an imperative sentence is in the base form.

> **Have** a cookie.   **Help** me.

indefinite article   The word *a* or *an. A/An* is used to introduce singular count nouns to a listener and/or a speaker.

> **a boy**   **an apple**

indirect object   A noun, pronoun, or noun phrase that indirectly receives the action of the verb in a sentence.

> Jack gave **Mary** a book.
> Mary bought **him** a new ring.

infinitive   *To* + the base form of a verb. Infinitives can be used as nouns.

> Peter loves **to work**.
> **To be** a ballet dancer is her dream.

information question   (See *wh-* question.)

intensifier   An adverb that makes the word it modifies stronger or weaker in meaning.

> I **really** love chocolate.
> He **hardly** thought about his decision.

intransitive verb   A verb that does not take an object.

> John **runs** every day.

linking verb   A verb that takes a subject complement. Linking verbs include *be, appear, feel, seem, smell,* and *become.*

> She **is** a teacher.   Ralph **feels** ill.

main clause (also called *independent clause*)   A clause that is or could be a complete sentence.

> **Today is Sunday.**
> When he called, **I wasn't home.**

main verb   The verb that can be used alone in a sentence in the simple present and simple past tense and that carries the primary verbal meaning in the sentence. Main verbs often occur with auxiliaries.

> Carol **ate** breakfast today.
> Carol has already **eaten**.

measure words   Quantifiers that express specific or exact amounts.

> **a cup of** sugar   **a loaf of** bread
> **two pounds of** apples

modal   An auxiliary verb used to express ability or possibility, ask for or give permission or advice, make offers and requests, or express necessity. Modals include *can, could, may, might, should, must, will,* and *would.*

> Harriet **can** speak French.
> You **should** learn Spanish.

modify   To tell more about or change the meaning of a word or phrase. For example, adjectives modify nouns.

> the **beautiful** woman

negative statement   A sentence that is not positive. Many negative statements contain *not.*

> I **do not like** chocolate.

noncount noun   A noun that names a person, place, thing, or idea that cannot be counted.

> **Mrs. Jones**   **Mel's Diner**
> **water**   **honesty**

noun   A word that names a person, place, thing, or idea.

> **king**   **New York City**   **house**   **love**

noun phrase   A noun and its modifiers.

> **the beautiful, big, blue ball on the table**

object of a preposition   A noun, pronoun, or noun phrase that comes after a preposition.

> from **Ben**   to **them**   at **the party**

particle   The adverb in a phrasal verb.

Please turn **off** the lights.

past progressive tense (also called *past continuous tense*)   A verb tense that describes actions in progress in the past.

At six o'clock last night, the sun **was shining**.

personal pronoun   A word that replaces a noun or noun phrase and functions as a subject, object, or subject complement in a sentence.

John is a teacher. **He** is a teacher.
Tim called Katy. Tim called **her**.
This is my car. This is **it**.

phrasal verb   A verb + adverb (particle) combination that has a special meaning. Some phrasal verbs take objects. Others do not take objects.

John has **made up** the exam.
I **work out** every day.

phrase   A group of related words that does not contain both a subject and a verb.

on the table   **the big, black dog**

plural   More than one. Pronouns and nouns can be plural (e.g., *they, we, two dogs*). Plural verb forms are used with plural subjects.

The **books are** on the table.

possessive   A noun (e.g., *John's*), pronoun (e.g., *mine*), or adjective (e.g., *my*) that shows ownership or possession.

John's car is new.   This book is **mine**.
This is **my** book.

predicate   The verb and the words that come after it in a statement.

I **like movies**.
Reza **has lived here for several years**.

preposition   A function word that takes a noun or pronoun as an object. Prepositions often express meanings like time, location, or direction.

at 10 o'clock   **in** the building
into the house

prepositional phrase   A preposition plus its object.

in the building   **into the house**

present perfect progressive tense (also called *present perfect continuous tense*)   A verb tense that describes actions in progress in the past which are continuing now or have just ended.

They **have been waiting** for over an hour.
Her eyes are red. She **has been crying**.

present perfect tense   A verb tense that describes actions and states that began in the past and continue to the present. The present perfect also describes actions and states completed at an indefinite time in the past.

Susan **has lived** here for 10 years.
Susan **has read** that book.

present progressive tense (also called *present continuous tense*)   A verb tense that describes actions happening at the moment of speaking or over a longer period of time in the present.

I **am writing** postcards right now.
We **are studying** English this semester.

pronoun   A word that replaces a noun or noun phrase (See *personal pronoun, possessive, reflexive pronoun*.)

John is my friend.   **He** is my friend.

proper noun   A noun that names a particular person, place, thing, or idea. Proper nouns begin with capital letters.

Mary Larson   **Paris**   **Christmas**

quantifier   A word or phrase that comes before a noun and tells *how many* or *how much*.

Many people enjoy walking.
They don't need **much** equipment to walk.

reflexive pronoun   A pronoun ending in *-self* or *-selves*. Reflexive pronouns are used when the subject and the object in a sentence are the same.

I hurt **myself**.
Angela bought **herself** a new bike.

short answer   An answer to a *yes/no* question that includes: *Yes/No*, + subject + auxiliary verb/*be* + (*not*).

> Do you like fish?   **No, I don't.**
> Are you tired?   **Yes, I am.**

simple past tense   A verb tense that describes actions and states that began and ended in the past.

> Plato **lived** in ancient Greece.
> John **was** here yesterday.

simple present tense   A verb tense that describes habits, routines, and things that are generally or always true.

> We often **meet** for breakfast.
> The earth **is** a planet.

singular   One. Pronouns and nouns can be singular (e.g., *I, she, book*). Singular verb forms are used with singular and noncount subjects.

> The **book is** on the table.
> The **sugar is** in the bowl.

stative meaning   States, not actions. Verbs with stative meaning do not usually occur in the progressive tenses.

> I **know** the answer.
> NOT: I am knowing the answer.

subject   The noun, pronoun, or noun phrase that comes before the verb in a statement. The subject is usually the doer of the action or the experiencer of the state in a sentence.

> **John** is a teacher.   **We** like chocolate.

subject complement   A noun, pronoun, noun phrase, or adjective that comes after *be* or another linking verb. A subject complement renames, identifies, or describes the subject of a sentence.

> Lois will become **a doctor** soon.
> John is **handsome.**

superlative   Form of an adjective or adverb used to compare three or more things or actions. Form of a noun or verb used to compare three or more quantities.

> The Nile is **the longest** river in the world.
> Jack exercises **the least** of all.

three-word verb   The combination of a phrasal verb + a preposition.

> I **met up with** Fred.
> He needs to **get down to** an exercise plan.

time clause   A clause that begins with a time expression (e.g., *when, while, before, as soon as, until, after*) and includes a subject and a verb.

> **When I ate**, I felt better.
> John's going to exercise **before he eats.**

transitive verb   A verb that can take an object.

> The dog **chased** the cat.

verb + preposition combination
A combination formed by certain verbs and certain prepositions. Prepositions in verb + preposition combinations often combine with verbs of thinking, speaking, sensing, or feeling. The preposition always has an object.

> He **thought of** a good idea.
> I was **talking to** my friend this morning.

yes/no question   A question that can be answered with *yes* or *no*.

> Yes/No Question: **Are you hungry?**
> Answer: Yes.

wh- question (also called *information question*) A question that begins with a *wh-* word (*who, what, where, when, why, how, how much, how many*) and asks for information. *Wh-* questions cannot usually be answered with only *yes* or *no*.

> Wh- question: **What do you want to eat?**
> Answer: A hamburger

Index

A

a. See Indefinite articles

Ability (*can, could, be able to*), 326–327

about, 204, 223

Active meaning. *See* Verbs, with active meaning

Adjectives, 240–241
comparative, 258–259
functions of, 240
-ing and *-ed* endings in, 246
nouns as, 240
possessive, 172, 181
prepositions and, 205, 209, 369, A-10–A-12
superlative, 264–265
word order of, 241

Adverbs, 193–194. *See also* Phrasal verbs
as . . . as with, 253
comparative, 258–259
of degree (intensifiers), 199, 203
of frequency, 13–14, 31, 198
of manner, 193, 199, A–10
of place, 193
of possibility, 198
superlative, 264–265
of time, 194

Advice expressions, 347–348, 355

a few, 158, 161

Affirmative statements
with *be*, A-1, A-6
future time expressions in, 89
indefinite pronouns in, 182
many in, 160
with modals, 319
in past progressive, 63
in present perfect, 277
in present perfect progressive, 300
in present progressive, 22–23
in simple past, 49, 57
in simple present, 5
some in, 161
with *will*, 97

afraid not, 338

after, 115–116, 204, 223

a great deal of, 158

a little, 158, 161

all, 158

almost, 199

almost always, 13

almost certainly, 330

almost certainly not, 330

a lot of, 158, 160

already, 290

always, 13, 100, 198

an. See Indefinite articles

Answers. *See* Short answers

any, 161

anybody, 182

anyone, 182

anything, 182

Apostrophe ('), 175

around, 205

Articles. *See* Definite article; Indefinite articles

as . . . as, 253–254

Asking permission expressions, 338

as soon as, 116

at, 204–205, 223

at (*specific clock time*), 49

at the moment, 20

Attitudes, expressions of, 34

Auxiliary verbs, 253, 258, 319. *See also be*; *do*; *have*; Modals

B

Background information, describing, 69

Base verbs, 5, 10, 22, 25–26, 49, 54, 57–58, 65–66, 89, 97–98, 319–321, 344, 365, 373, 385. *See also* Verbs

be, 13, 22, 25, 26, 63, 65, 89, 94, 175, 182, 240–241, 300–301, 304, 321, 365, 373, A-1, A-6

been, 300–301, 304

before, 116, 204

begin, 386

be going to, 89, 94, 105–106, 108, 122

Belief, modals of, 330–331

be used to, 385

-body ending, 182

bunches, 167

by, 174, 204

C

can, 319–321, 326–327, 329, 338–339, 341

cannot, 319, 320, 330

can't, 319, 320, 329

Capitalization, 138–139

certainly, 98, 198, 335

certainly not, 330

Clauses
adverb position in, 194
future time, 115–116
if, 122–123
main, 73, 75, 115–116, 122–123
negative, 115
order of, 115–116, 122
past time, 73–75, 79–80, 285

cloves, 167

Commas,
between adjectives, 241
after *if* clauses, 122
after time clauses, 73, 115

Common nouns, 138–139

Comparative adjectives and adverbs, 258–259, A-12

Comparison
with *as . . . as*, 253–254
with comparative adjectives and adverbs, 258–259, A-12
with superlative adjectives and adverbs, 264–265, A-12

Conditionals. *See* Factual conditionals; Future conditionals; Negative conditionals

Consonants, articles and, 148

continue, 386

Contractions, 25–26
in future time expressions, 89
of *had better*, 355
of indefinite pronouns, 183
with modals, 320–321
in present perfect, 277, 280
in present perfect progressive, 300–301
in present progressive, 22
in simple past, 49, 54, 57, 60
of *wh-* words, 28
of *will*, 97, 99, 101

could, 319–320, 326–327, 330–331, 335, 338–339, 341, 344, 348
could not, 330
Count nouns, 141–142, 149, 158, 160, 167, A-7

D

Days of week, 139
Decisions, expressions of, 100, 106
Definite article (*the*), 138, 151, 210
definitely, 98, 198, 335
Degree, adverbs of (intensifiers), 199, 203
Descriptions, expressions of, 34
did, 49, 54, 57–58, 60
"*didja*", 60
did not, 49, 57
didn't, 49, 54, 57
Direction adverbs, 193
Direct objects, A-9. *See also* Objects
do, 5, 9–10, 49, 54, 57, 60, 246, 253, 258, 344
does, 9–10, 246
does not, 5, 9
doesn't, 5, 9
do not, 5, 9
don't, 5, 9
don't have to, 348, 350
down, 205, 215, 223
during, 204

E

each and every, 158
-*ed* endings, 49, 246, A-11–A-12
Emotions, expressions of, 34, 246
enough, 158, 161, 199
-*er* endings, 258
-*es* endings, 6, 10
-*est* endings, 264
ever, 14, 290, 291
every, 158, 161
everybody, 182
every day, 31
everyone, 182
everything, 182
Expectations, expressions of, 89, 105
extremely, 199

F

Factual conditionals, 122–123
Feelings, expressions of, 223, 246
few, 158, 161, 290

for, 49, 204, 223, 285, 301, 308, 378
forget, 386
Frequency, adverbs of, 13–14, 31, 198
frequently, 13
from, 204–205, 223
f sound, as word ending, 168
Future conditionals, 122–123
Future possibility, 335
Future time clauses, 115
    questions in, 116
    simple present in, 115
    statements in, 115
    time expressions in, 115–116
Future time, 89
    in affirmative statements, 89
    with *be going to*, 89, 94
    be going to versus *will* in, 105–106
    conditionals in, 122–123
    contractions in, 89
    immediate expectations, 89
    in negative statements, 89
    plans, 89
    predictions, 89
    present progressive *versus* simple present for, 107–108
    with *will*, 97–100

G

Gerunds, 365–366
    after *go*, 369
    after prepositions, 369
    function of, 365–366
    progressive verbs *versus*, 369
    verbs before, A-13
Gerunds *versus* infinitives, 383
    be used to and, 385
    forget, *remember*, and *stop*, 386
    prepositions and, 383
    same and different meanings of, 386
    verbs and, 383
Giving permission expressions, 338
go, 369. *See also* be going to
go ahead, 338
"*gonna*," 94
good, 241
Groups, 141, A–8

H

h, articles with, 149
had better, 320, 355

had better not, 355
hard, 199
hardly, 199
hardly ever, 13–14
has, 277, 280, 282, 300–301, 304, 321
has not, 277
hasn't, 277
hate, 386
have, 35, 277, 280, 282, 300–301, 304, 321
have a good time, 35
have a problem, 35
have dinner, 35
have not, 277
haven't, 277
have to, 330
have trouble, 35
he, 172
heads, 167
her, 172
herself, 172
him, 172
himself, 172
his, 172
how, 26, 54, 66, 94, 193
how long, 282, 304
how many, 160
how much, 160
how often, 10, 13, 198, 282, 304
how sure, 198

I

I, 172
Ideas, expressions of, 34
-*ies* endings, 6
if clauses, 122–123
Imperatives
    orders as, 355
    requests as, 344
in, 204–205, 223
Indefinite articles (*a, an*), 138, 148–149, 210
Indefinite pronouns, 182–183
Indirect objects, A–9. *See also* Objects
Infinitives, 373–374. *See also* Gerunds *versus* infinitives
    it and, 375
    negative, 373
    of purpose, 378
    as subjects, 373
    verbs and, 373–374, A-13
in front of, 204

-ing endings, 22, 65, 66, 246, 300–301, 304, A-2, A-11–A-12
in order + infinitive, 378
Intensifiers (adverbs), 199, 203
into, 205
Irregular comparatives, 259
Irregular noun forms, 141
Irregular past participles, 277
Irregular plural nouns, 141
Irregular superlatives, 265
Irregular verbs, 49, A-4–A-5
it, 172, 373, 375
I think, 98
its, 172
itself, 172

J

ja, 60
just, 253, 290, 294

K

kind of, 203

L

last (*specific time of day*), 49
least, 264–265
less, 258
let's, 320, 357
like, 204, 386
Linking verbs, 240–241
Listening for *can* and *can't*, 329
little, 158, 161
loaves, 167
Location adverbs, 193
lots of, 158, 160
love, 386

M

Main clauses, 73, 75, 115–116, 122–123
Manner, adverbs of, 193, 199, A-10
many, 160, 161, 290
Mass nouns, 141. *See also* Noncount nouns
may, 319, 330–331, 335, 338–339
maybe, 98, 198, 330–331
may be, 331
maybe not, 330, 335
may not, 320, 330, 335
me, 172
Measure words, 167–168, 259
might, 319, 330–331, 335, 348
might not, 330, 335

mine, 172
Modal-like expressions, 320, 355
Modals, 319–321. *See also* Social modals
  of ability, 326–327
  affirmative statements with, 319, 321
  of belief, 330–331
  of future possibility, 335
  negative statements with, 319, 321
  phrasal, 321
  of present possibility, 330–331
  short answers with, 319, 321
  wh- questions in, 320–321
  yes/no questions with, 319, 321
Modifying
  by adjectives, 240
  by adverbs, 193
Months of year, 139
more, 258
most, 158, 264–265
most of the time, 31
much, 158, 160, 161
must, 319, 330
must not, 330, 348, 350
my, 172
myself, 172

N

near, 204
nearly, 253
Necessity expressions, 347
Negative conditionals, 122
Negative infinitives, 373
Negative statements
  any in, 161
  with *be*, A-1, A-6
  future time expressions in, 89
  indefinite pronouns in, 182
  many and *much* in, 160
  in modals, 321
  with modals, 319
  in past progressive, 63
  in present perfect, 277, 290–291
  in present perfect progressive, 301
  in present progressive, 22
  in simple past, 49, 57
  in simple present, 5
  with *will*, 97
never, 13–15, 100, 198, 290
no, 158, 161
nobody, 182

Noncount nouns, 141–142, 149, 151, 158, 160, 167, A-8–A-9
none, 158
Non-necessity expressions, 347
no one, 182
not, 182
not as . . . as, 253
nothing, 182
Nouns, 138–139
  as adjectives, 240
  common, 138–139
  comparing, 253
  count, 141–142
  definite article and, 151
  functions of, A–9
  gerunds as, 365
  indefinite articles and, 148–149
  infinitives as, 373–374
  irregular plural, A–8
  noncount, 141–142, A-8–A-9
  numbers with, 167
  as objects of phrasal verbs, 215
  plural, 141
  plural count, A–7
  possessive, 175
  pronouns from, 172–175
  proper, 138–139
  quantifiers with, 158, 160–161
  singular, 141
now, 20, 31
Numbers, 167–168

O

Objects
  gerunds as, 366, 369
  nouns as, A–9
  phrasal verbs and, 215
  pronouns as, 173–174, 193, 204, 254, 262
  in verb-preposition combinations, 223
Obligation expressions, 347
occasionally, 13
of, 168, 204, 223
of course, 338
off, 205, 215, 223
Offers, expressions of, 106, 339
often, 13, 198
okay, 338
on, 31, 49, 204–205, 223
-one ending, 182
one of the . . ., 265

One-word modals, 319. *See also* Modals

onto, 205

on top of, 204

Opinion, expressions of, 348

Order
of adjectives, 241
of clauses, 116
of words, 116, 122, 241, 244

Order, imperatives as, 355

ought to, 320, 330, 348

our, 172

ours, 172

ourselves, 172

out, 215, 223

out of, 205

over, 205

Ownership, expressions of, 34–35

P

Particles. *See* Phrasal verbs

Past participles, 277, 290

Past progressive, 63
affirmative statements in, 63
function of, 63
negative statements in, 63
past time clauses and, 73–75
short answers in, 65
simple past tense *versus*, 68–69, 73–75
wh- questions in, 65
yes/no questions in, 65

Past tense. *See* Simple past

Past time clauses, 73–75, 285

perhaps, 198, 330, 335

perhaps not, 330, 335

Permission, expressions for, 338

Personal pronouns, 172

Phrasal modals, 321

Phrasal verbs, 215–216
meanings of, A-10–A-11
objects with, 215
as three-word verbs, 229
verb-preposition combinations *versus*, 223, 228–229

Place expressions, 193, 205

Plans, expressions of, 89, 105, 107–108

please, 341

plenty, 158, 161

Plural nouns, 141–142, 149, 151, 158, 167, A-7–A-8

Politeness, 224, 338

Possession, expressions of, 34–35

Possessive adjectives, 172–174
nouns as, 175
pronouns as, 172–174

Possibility
adverbs of, 198
future, 335
present, 330–331

possibly, 198, 330, 335, 341

possibly not, 330, 335

Predictions, expressions of, 89, 98, 105, 107–108

prefer, 386

Prepositions and prepositional phrases. *See also* Verb-preposition combinations
adjectives ending in *-ed* and, 246
adjectives with, 205, A-10–A-12
articles and, 210
gerunds after, 369
gerunds *versus* infinitives and, 383
objects of, 173, A–9
of place, 205
after superlatives, 265
of time, 204

Present continuous. *See* Present progressive

Present perfect, 277
in affirmative statements, 277
already and *yet* in, 290
contractions in, 277, 280
ever and *never* in, 290
few, many, and *several* in, 290
indefinite past and, 285
in negative statements, 277
present perfect progressive *versus*, 307–308
recently and *just* in, 290
of regular and irregular verbs, 277
short answers in, 282
simple past *versus*, 294
for and *since* in, 285
time expressions in, 290–291
wh- questions in, 282
yes/no questions in, 282

Present perfect continuous. *See* Present perfect progressive

Present perfect progressive, 300–301
affirmative statements in, 300
function of, 301
negative statements in, 301
present perfect *versus*, 307–308

short answers in, 304
time expressions in, 301
wh- questions in, 304
yes/no questions in, 304

Present possibility, 330–331

Present progressive, 20
affirmative statements in, 22
contractions in, 28
for future time expressions, 107–108
negative statements in, 22
short answers in, 25–26
simple present *versus*, 31
verbs with active meaning and, 34
wh- questions in, 26
yes/no questions in, 25

Present tense. *See* Simple present

pretty, 203

probably, 98, 198, 330, 335

probably not, 330, 335

Prohibition expressions, 347

Promises, expressions of, 100, 106

Pronouns, 172–175
indefinite, 182–183
infinitives with, 373–374
as objects, 193, 204, 254, 262
as objects of phrasal verbs, 215, 223
possessive adjectives and, 172–174
as subjects, 254, 262
will and, 101

Pronunciation
of *did* in simple past, 60
of regular plural count nouns, A-7
of regular verbs in simple past, A-3
of simple past, 49
of third person singular, A-2

Proper nouns, 138–139

Purpose, infinitives of, 378

Q

Quantifiers, 158
with comparatives, 259
enough and *plenty* as, 161
a few and *a little* as, 161
few and *little* as, 161
measure words as, 167–168
much and *many* as, 160
numbers as, 167–168
some and *any* as, 160–161
too much and *too many* as, 161

Questions. *See also wh-* questions;
    yes/no questions
    in future time clauses, 116
    indefinite pronouns in, 182
    in present perfect, 290–291
quite, 199, 203

R

rarely, 13–14
really, 199, 203
recently, 290, 294
Reflexive pronouns, 172, 174
Refusals, expressions of, 106, 338
Regular verbs, 49
remember, 386
Requests, expressions of, 100, 106,
    341
right now, 20

S

Scenes, describing, 69
Schedules, expressions for, 107
Seasons of year, 139
seldom, 13–15, 198
-s endings, 6, 10, 141, 175, A-2
Sensing, expressions of, 34, 223
Sentences
    conditionals in, 122–123
    with past time clauses, 73–75
    subjects of, 26, 54, 94, 319–320
    writing, 24–25
several, 158, 290
she, 172
Short answers
    with *be*, A-1, A-6
    with *be going to*, 94
    with modals, 321
    in past progressive, 65
    in present perfect, 282
    in present progressive, 25–26
    in simple past, 54
    in simple present, 9–10
    with *will*, 99
should, 319–321, 330, 335, 348
should not, 330, 335
Simple past, 49
    affirmative statements in, 49, 57
    of *be*, A-6
    contractions and, 60
    function of, 49
    negative statements in, 49, 57
    past progressive *versus*, 68–69,
        73–75
    present perfect *versus*, 294

pronunciation of, 49
regular and irregular verbs in,
    49
short answers in, 54
spelling rules for regular verbs
    in, A-3
in time clauses, 285
used to and, 57–58
wh- questions in, 54, 58, 60
yes/no questions in, 54
Simple present, 5–6
    adverbs of frequency with, 13–14
    affirmative statements in, 5
    of *be*, A–1
    function of, 5
    in future time clauses, 115–116
    in future time expressions,
        107–108
    in *if* clauses, 122–123
    negative statements in, 5
    present progressive *versus*, 31
    pronunciation of third person
        singular form of, A-2
    in short answers, 9–10
    spelling rules for, 6
    third person singular in, 6
    verbs with stative meaning
        and, 34
wh- questions in, 10
yes/no questions in, 9
since, 285, 301, 308
Singular nouns, 141–142, 149,
    151, 158, 167
so, 199, 203
Social modals, 338–339
    advice expressions as, 347–348
    for asking, giving, and refusing
        permission, 338–339
    imperative orders *versus*, 355
    imperative requests *versus*, 344
    necessity expressions as, 347,
        349–351
    for offering, 339
    opinion expressions as, 348
    for politeness, 338
    for requesting, 341
    suggestion expressions as, 357
some, 158, 161
somebody, 182
someone, 182
something, 182
sometimes, 13, 198
Speaking
    articles in, 149, 151

contractions in, 101
ending *f* sound, 168
plural pronouns in, 183
stress placement in, 229
verb-preposition combinations
    and, 223
Spelling rules
    for adverbs of manner, A-10
    of *-ing* verb forms, A-2
    for regular plural count nouns,
        A-7
    for simple past, 49, A-3
    for simple present, 6
start, 386
Statements, 115. *See also*
    Affirmative statements;
    Negative statements
States of being, 34–35, 68
Stative meaning. *See* Verbs, with
    stative meaning
stop, 386
Stories, 69
Stress placement, 229
Subjects
    gerunds as, 365
    infinitives as, 373
    nouns as, A-9
    pronouns as, 173–175, 254, 262
    of sentences, 26, 54, 94, 319–320
Suggestion, expressions of, 357
Superlative adjectives and
    adverbs, 264–265, A-12
sure, 338

T

than, 258–259
the. *See* Definite articles
their, 172, 183
theirs, 172
them, 172, 183
themselves, 172
these days, 20, 31
they, 172, 183
-thing ending, 182
Thinking, expressions of, 223
Third person singular, 6, A-2
this (*specific time of day*), 49
this (*specific time term*), 31
this year, 20
Three-word verbs, 229, A-11
through, 205
Time clauses, 73–75, 115–116,
    285. *See also* Future time
    clauses; Past time clauses

Time expressions, 31
  in adverbs, 194
  in future time clauses, 115–116
  in past progressive, 63
  in prepositions and
    prepositional phrases, 204
  in present perfect, 290–291
  in present perfect progressive,
    301
  in present progressive, 20
  in simple past, 49
  with *will*, 100
to, 204–205, 223, 229, 321
today, 20, 31
tonight, 31
too, 199
too many, 161
too much, 161
Two-word verbs. *See* Phrasal verbs

U

Uncountable nouns, 141. *See also*
  Noncount nouns
under, 204
until, 116, 204
up, 205, 215, 223
us, 172
use, 58
used to, 57–58
"*useta*," 60
usually, 13, 198

V

Verb-preposition combinations,
  223, A-11
  phrasal verbs *versus*, 223,
    228–229
  stress placement for, 232
  three-word verbs as, 229
Verbs. *See also* Future
    conditionals; Past progressive;
    Phrasal verbs; Present perfect;
    Present perfect progressive;
    Present progressive; Simple
    past; Simple present
  with active meaning, 34–35
  as adjectives, 246
  adverbs for, 13, 193, 198
  after *as . . . as*, 253
  after *than*, 258
  agreement with indefinite
    pronouns, 182

  auxiliary, 253, 258, 319. *See also*
    be; *do*; *have*; Modals
  base, 5, 10, 22, 25–26, 49, 54,
    57–58, 65–66, 89, 97–98,
    319–321, 344, 365, 373, 385
  be. *See be*
  for count and noncount nouns,
    142
  with gerunds, A-13
  gerunds *versus* infinitives with,
    383
  imperative, 344
  infinitives and, 373–374, A-13
  irregular, 49, A-4–A-5
  linking, 240–241
  objects of, 173
  pairs of, to express future time,
    107
  present perfect of, 277
  progressive, gerunds *versus*, 369
  regular, 49
  simple past, A-3
  with stative meaning, 34–35, 69,
    241, 308
  third person singular form of, 6
  three-word, 229
very, 199, 203
Vowels, articles and, 148

W

Warning expressions, 355
was, A-6
we, 172
well, 241
were, A-6
what, 10, 26, 54, 58, 66, 94, 99,
  282, 304, 320
when, 10, 58, 66, 73–75, 99,
  115–116, 194, 321
where, 10, 26, 54, 66, 99, 193, A-1,
  A-6
while, 73–74
who, 10, 26, 54, 58, 94, 99, 282,
  304, 320, A-1, A-6
whom, 10, 26, 54, 282, 304
wh- questions
  any in, 161
  with *be*, A-1, A-6
  with *be going to*, 94
  contractions in, 28
  many and *much* in, 160
  in modals, 320–321

  in past progressive, 65
  in present perfect, 282
  in present progressive, 26
  in simple past, 54, 58, 60
  in simple present, 10
  with *will*, 99
why, 304, 378
will, 97–100, 122, 319, 335, 339,
  341
  affirmative statements with, 97
  be going to versus, 105–106
  contractions with, 99, 101
  negative statements with, 97
  predictions with, 98
  short answers with, 99
  time expressions with, 100
  wh- questions with, 99
  yes/no questions with, 99
will not, 97
with, 204, 229
won't, 97–99
Words
  f sound at end of, 168
  measure, 167–168, 259
  order of, 116, 122, 241
would, 319, 341, 344
Writing
  contractions in, 101
  ending *f* sound, 168
  plural pronouns, 183
  sentences, 24–25

Y

yes/no questions
  any in, 161
  with *be*, A-1, A-6
  with *be going to*, 94
  many and *much* in, 160
  with modals, 321
  in past progressive, 65
  in present perfect, 282
  in present progressive, 25
  in simple past, 54
  in simple present, 9
  with *will*, 99
yesterday, 49
yet, 290–291
you, 172, 344
your, 172
yours, 172
yourself, 172